The Place of the Gospels
in the General History
of Literature

The Place of the Gospels
in the General History
of Literature

Karl Ludwig Schmidt

Translated by Byron R. McCane
with an introduction by John Riches

UNIVERSITY OF SOUTH CAROLINA PRESS

Published in Columbia, South Carolina, by the
University of South Carolina Press

Manufactured in the United States of America

06   05   04   03   02   5   4   3   2   1

Library of Congress Cataloging-in-Publication Data

Schmidt, Karl Ludwig, 1891–
  [Stellung der Evangelien in der allgemeinen Literaturgeschichte. English]
  The place of the Gospels in the general history of literature / Karl Ludwig
Schmidt ; translated by Byron R. McCane ; with an introduction by John Riches.
     p. cm.
Includes bibliographical references and index.
  ISBN 1-57003-430-3 (cloth : alk. paper)
  1. Bible. N.T. Gospels—Criticism, interpretation, etc. I. Title.
  BS2555.52 .S413 2002
  226'.066—dc21   2002012310

Contents

Introduction: Karl Ludwig Schmidt's *The Place of the Gospels in the General History of Literature*
JOHN RICHES   vii
Translator's Introduction   xxix
Acknowledgments   xxxv

PART ONE   Description and critique of previous attempts to determine the place of the gospels in the general history of literature   1

1. Greek biographical literature: Lives of philosophers, Diogenes Laertius, contemporaneous historiography, Xenophon's *Memorabilia* (Jesus and Socrates, Justin and the gospels, Papias and the gospels, Justin and Papias), Peripatetic and Alexandrian biography.   3
2. Judaism and Hellenism, Aramaic folk books, ancient and modern Orientalia, Rabbinics, the Hebrew Bible.   14
3. Low literature from various periods and peoples.   19
4. Analogy, not genealogy; Gospels and Jewish apocalyptic?   25

PART TWO   The place of the gospels in the general history of literature   27

1. The literary development of the noncanonical acts, (literary) lives of saints and martyr-acts; the passion narrative of Jesus; gospels and the formation of the canon.   29
2. Gospels and biography: arrangement of the material, portraiture, the problem of truth-content.   32
3. The boundary between high literature and low literature: the gospels and Philostratus' *Life of Apollonius of Tyana*.   34
4. Simple cases of folk biography: *Littérature orale*.   37
5. Methodology: literary criticism and style criticism (form criticism).   39
6. The multiformity of the framework of the story of Jesus; *Chreia*-traditions.   43
7. German folk books: *Doktor Faust*.   45
8. Legends of the saints.   52
9. Ancient Christian monastic stories: *Historia Monachorum* and *Historia Lausiaca; Apophthegmata Patrum*.   55
10. The Franciscan legends.   60
11. Goethe and the legends of St. Rochus; Martin Buber and the Hasidic legends of the Great Maggid.   65
12. The cultic character of legends of saints, *Apophthegmata Patrum*, and the gospels.   68

PART THREE   On the problem of the literary character of the gospels: The history of religions and theological question.   77

Index   87

INTRODUCTION

Karl Ludwig Schmidt's *The Place of the Gospels in the General History of Literature*

JOHN RICHES

The appearance in English, nearly eighty years after its first publication, of one of the major works of early-twentieth-century German gospel criticism, represents yet another triumph of the persistence of the few over the indifference and hostility of the many. In this way, Schmidt's article in the *Eucharisterion* Festschrift joins William Wrede's *Messianic Secret* (1901; 1971)[1] and Rudolf Bultmann's *History of the Synoptic Tradition* (1921; 1961)[2] as works that have waited too long before they were made available to those without easy access to German. This leaves Schmidt's own *Der Rahmen der Geschichte Jesu*[3] as the last of the major works of the form critics still to be translated. Is this too little too late, or is there still an opportunity for a serious reappraisal of the work of the form critics?

It is hard not to see an underlying theological tendency behind the English-speaking world's resistance to the works of Wrede and the form critics. Both, in different ways, posed a challenge to the recognition of Mark as a reliable source for the life of Jesus. The recognition of Markan priority, which was given almost canonical status by Streeter's *The Four Gospels*,[4] appeared to provide scholars with the earliest (and therefore?) most trustworthy source for the life of Jesus.[5] Wrede's uncovering of deep-seated theological motifs in the presentation of Jesus in the gospels posed questions about the objectivity of their account of Jesus' life and indeed about the reliability of the knowledge it could provide of Jesus' own self-consciousness. It was the fact that the "messianic secret" (whether attributed to the early Christian tradition or to Mark)[6] was presented by Wrede as having been added to the tradition that caused offense to many in the English-speaking world.

Wrede, quite properly, saw his own inquiry as continuous with the work of the source critics. If they had battled long and hard to determine the priority of the gospels and so to distinguish later literary developments from earlier, he would undertake the same task for the gospel tradition and attempt to discern later additions to the tradition, such as the cluster of motifs he identified as the messianic secret. This proved one step too far for the theological (and aesthetic) tastes of scholars like William Sanday.[7] Sanday saw Wrede's book as a direct attack on the gospel regarded by most scholars as "the foundation for their reconstruction of the Life of Christ."[8] His review is a strange mixture of fascination and distaste. He cannot but be interested in the way Wrede combines the various motifs of the "secret" into a single whole; he lampoons the cast of mind that refuses to consider that there may be still some explanation of the facts that would allow them to form part of the life of Jesus.[9] Yet, while the form critics certainly made it difficult to regard the gospels any longer as "foundational for the reconstruction of the Life of Christ," their work still stood in the service of the quest of the historical Jesus.

Whether it was Bultmann's attempt to identify the theological tendencies that shaped the synoptic tradition or, as we shall see in more detail, Schmidt's account of the framework of the gospel narrative, such works combined to demonstrate that the gospels were the receptors into which a lively and developing tradition had flowed. The gospels, that is to say, were not simple historical accounts. The great discovery of the form critics was the transparency of the gospels to the oral tradition. The chronological and topographical outline of Mark's gospel, Schmidt argued, was largely the product of the simple juxtaposition of traditional units of material, each of which brought with it its own particular framework. The resultant outline of Jesus' life was neither particularly coherent nor, indeed, historically trustworthy. Luke attempted to remove some of the contradictions and confusions; Matthew largely abandoned the attempt and rearranged much of the material topically. Thus, the work of the evangelists, even of Luke, largely respects the traditional material they inherited. It is, however, one thing to show that the evangelists handled the tradition with respect; it is another to show that the synoptic tradition is an adequate "foundation for the reconstruction of the Life of Christ."

Certainly, the form critics in the 1920s continued to take a lively interest in the quest for the historical Jesus. Bultmann wrote his *Jesus* as a contribution to a popular series whose title echoed Carlyle, *Die Unsterblichen: Die Geistigen Heroen der Menschheit in ihrem Leben und Wirken;*[10] Schmidt contributed the article on Jesus Christ to the second edition of *Die Religion in Geschichte und Gegenwart.*[11] Despite this, it is the negative implications of their work that are best known. Bultmann is presented as historically skeptical, despite his Jesus book, which portrays Jesus as an existential prophet.[12] Indeed, later it was often said that Bultmann's form-critical work had made it impossible to continue studies of the historical Jesus. But Bultmann's turning away from such work had theological rather than historical reasons.[13] Ultimately, his theological sympathies lay with (as he saw it) the fourth evangelist's existential reworking of the tradition, rather than with the mythologizing tendencies of the synoptic tradition, which he had attempted to uncover.

Schmidt's work on the narrative framework of the gospels is usually (and, indeed, correctly) presented as making it impossible to write a life of Jesus, in the sense that it is now no longer possible to speak with any confidence about developments that may have occurred in the course of his life. This was perfectly clear to Schmidt himself, but it did not lead him to conclude that therefore there is nothing at all to be said about Jesus' life. What the gospels would not provide was a portrait of Jesus. But this did not mean that scholars were unable to reconstruct the main characteristics of his teaching and deeds, and such reconstructions would allow for assessment of Jesus' demand that his followers confess him as the messianic Son of God. The work of the form critics, that is to say, did not fundamentally undermine the quest for the historical Jesus. What it did was to undermine accounts of his life that were based principally on a fairly straight-forward reading of Mark's gospel.

The works of the form critics were largely neglected in the early years in the English-speaking world—certainly they were not translated in the 1920s—and it was only gradually that discussions began to appear[14] that were in a mea-sure sympathetic to form criticism while retaining an interest in the historical Jesus. Notable among these was that of C.H. Dodd, who in his *Parables of the Kingdom* sought to get behind the traditional applications of the parables that were to be found in the gospels to their original form and setting.[15] Dodd's book was immensely influential, and his views continued to receive widespread acclaim well into the 1960s.[16] Thus, if only indirectly, the influence of the form critics was in due course strongly felt. By the 1960s discussions of the methods of establishing the authenticity of Jesus' sayings had become well established. Bultmann's *History of the Synoptic Tradition* had at last been translated, and the view that the evangelists were largely collectors of the tradition who had "strung pearls on a string" had gained wide currency.[17] A major influence here was Den-nis Nineham's commentary on Mark,[18] which introduced the work of the form critics to a wider audience and which still remains influential. At the same time, the work of German redaction critics such as Marxsen, Bornkamm, Conzel-mann, and Schweizer—which was quickly translated and adopted by English-speaking critics—was firmly based on the work of the form critics, even if it would begin to pose a challenge to the understanding of the role of the evange-lists that the form critics had championed. Again, among English-speaking scholars there were very different measures of acceptance of the form-critical assumptions that were shared by German redaction critics. Ernest Best's detailed studies of discipleship in Mark provide a fine example of a redaction criticism firmly grounded in a study of the tradition history of each pericope.[19] For the most part, however, redaction critics made sparing use of tradition-historical and form-critical studies; there was a preference for the notion of composition criti-cism, which gave greater attention to the overall design of the gospels.[20]

Thus, a gradual sea change has occurred over the last twenty years, which has seen the brief period of English-speaking scholars' engagement with the work of the form critics yield, with an almost audible sigh of relief, to one in which attention can again focus on the work of the evangelists. As we shall see in more detail later, this shift of focus has been a subtle one. It moves from the solid ground of claiming that the evangelists have, in varying ways, an active role in the ordering and redacting of the gospel material; to seeing them as authors in their own right; to comparisons between the evangelists and the writers of ancient biographies/lives. Thus a movement within the discipline that has firm roots within the tradition of form-critical studies of the gospels ends up, by a strange sleight of hand, by denying its origins. One might have expected a fuller account of this act of parricide; in practice what is offered is usually no more than the briefest dismissal of the main tenets of the form critics with little attention to the wealth of detailed argument with which they were supported. Thus, Richard Burridge[21] focuses his criticism on four main claims:

1. The form critics, we are reminded, distinguished *Hochliteratur* from *Kleinliteratur,* with the Gospels belonging to the latter category. "The two types of literature are seen in very rigid terms—and ne'er the twain shall meet. Any attempt to ask literary questions about the gospels, and in particular, their genre, is automatically precluded in advance."[22]

2. A related point is made against Bultmann that he "concluded that no analogy was necessary for this [the form of the gospel], since it was merely a by-product of the collecting together of the individual units with the oral tradition."[23] But, it is suggested, this fails to take into account that even collectors may work very differently with the material once gathered.

3. This "approach led to the eclipse of the author . . . the evangelist is seen as little more than a mere stenographer at the end of the oral tunnel."[24] Any consideration of the evangelists' intention or purpose is precluded.

4. The "form-critical view emphasized the unique character of the gospels. This may have had important theological implications for Bultmann and others as befitting the narrative of the unique proclamation of the gospel, but from a literary point of view, it is a nonsense."[25] There is no such thing as a literary novelty or unique kind of writing, and if there were, it would not be intelligible to anyone.

One may observe that it is prima facie strange, to say the very least, that someone who apparently believed that the gospels were without parallel in the world of literature should have written a major essay with the title "The Position of the Gospels in the General History of Literature." It suggests that he wished neither to make a wholly absolute distinction between the *Kleinliteratur,* to which he believed the gospels to belong, and other more consciously literary forms of writing, nor to dispute that the gospels could be categorized within that history. Whether or not he thought this precluded discussions of purpose and intentionality, we shall have to see. In any case, a proper response to such charges as those of Burridge requires, first, a fuller account of Schmidt's major work. Only then will we attempt a fuller response to those who now argue vigorously for seeing the gospels as forms of ancient biography. But first, a brief account of Schmidt's life.

Karl-Ludwig Schmidt was born on February 5, 1891, the son of a shoemaker in Frankfurt. Despite the economic and social hardships of his circumstances, he made his way successfully from the Lessing Gymnasium in Frankfurt to university studies. He first studied classical philology at Marburg (1909) and then embarked on the study of theology, probably at the suggestion of Martin Rade, the liberal theologian who edited *Die Christliche Welt.* He completed his studies in Berlin, where Adolf Deissmann was the teacher who most influenced him. He took his doctorate in 1913 with a study on *The Problem of the Unity of the Gospel of John with Particular Reference to Recent Interpolation Hypotheses* and became Deissmann's *Assistent.* In 1915 he was called up, and he was seriously wounded in September on the Polish front. After his discharge from the army, he took his church examinations and completed his practical training. In 1918 he took his *Habilitation,* with his *Der Rahmen der Geschichte Jesu: Literarkritische Untersuchungen zur ältesten Jesusüberlieferung.*[26] The book is dedicated to Deissmann.

Schmidt remained in Berlin as a *Privatdozent* until 1921, when he moved to a chair at Giessen. In 1925 he moved to Jena and from thence, in 1929, to Bonn. In 1933, as the Nazis came to power, he stood as the SPD candidate in the local government elections in Bonn. Though elected, he was prevented by the Nazis from taking up his seat. On September 15, 1933, he was dismissed from his chair after a campaign against him was initiated by the German Christians (a church group closely allied to the Nazis). In November 1933 he emigrated to Switzerland, where he was elected to a chair in Basel in 1935. In 1937 he was forced by the Nazis to give up the editorship of the journal, *Theologische Blätter,* which he had founded in 1922. In 1939 he was stripped of his German citizenship. He suffered a stroke in 1952 while lecturing in Basel, retired on grounds of ill-health in 1953, and died on January 10, 1956.

Schmidt's early works—his doctorate, *Habilitation,* and the present essay—are all works of *Literarkritik.* His primary concern in these studies is with the relation between the gospels and the oral tradition they set down and, in consequence, with the question, What sort of books are they? To say this is to make the point that the present essay, with its attempt to find analogies for the gospels in a wide sweep of literary history, is closely related to, and can scarcely be appreciated without a clear understanding of, Schmidt's work in *Der Rahmen der Geschichte Jesu.* It is in that work, with its detailed consideration of the chronological and topographical framing of individual pericopes and complexes of pericopes, that the groundwork for the views in the present essay is laid.

Yet, while Schmidt's works are indeed all primarily literary—concerned, that is, to cast light on the processes whereby the gospels reached their present form and hence to shed light on the nature of that form—they are situated within a wider debate that is historical in character. The immediate context is a debate about the relative merits of the synoptic and Johannine chronologies, which was pursued rather differently among Catholic and Protestant scholars. Was the synoptic chronology, which suggested a ministry of no more than a year, most of which was conducted in Galilee, or the Johannine, with a longer ministry of up to three years, much of which is set in Jerusalem and its environs, to be preferred as giving the correct outline of Jesus' life?

In his interesting discussion of the history of this question, which includes gospel harmonies in the early church, Schmidt remarks how widespread was the view in the early period that the gospels contained loosely arranged material whose order was not that of *rerum gestarum* but of *recordationis*—the order not in which they had occurred but in which they were remembered.[27] More recent Catholic discussion had, however, been "more papal than the pope" and had sought to advance the claims of either John or the Synoptics as offering the true historical account of Jesus' life. Instructively, in the process of the heated debate that ensued, powerful arguments were forged against the chronological and topographical coherence of both the Synoptic Gospels and John by scholars who sought to advance the claims of one gospel's chronology by traducing the historical accuracy of another. Schmidt sought to build on this close literary analysis of the gospel narratives by looking in detail at the manner in which the individual pericopes in the gospels were framed, seeking to demonstrate that the chronological and topographical elements are no more than frames for originally independent stories about Jesus, designed principally for reception within the worshiping community of the early church.[28] It is worth citing his conclusion in full:

The Framework (Rahmen) *of the Story of Jesus in Mark, Matthew, and Luke.*

The earliest outline (*Aufriss*) of the story of Jesus is that of the Gospel of Mark. The inconsistencies in the traditions it contains show us what the earliest Jesus tradition looked like: there was no continuous narrative, but an abundance of individual stories, which for the most part are arranged topically. The precise nature of these topics is not always clear because they are linked to the history of primitive Christianity with its different religious, apologetic, and missionary interests. Luke is also a part of the process, though he is the only evangelist who additionally has literary aspirations. But this means that he is not able to do justice to the true nature of the gospel tradition, with its self-contained pericopes, which were primarily intended for use in Christian worship. The church took Matthew as its favorite gospel, the gospel, that is to say, which even more than Mark sought to offer a topical arrangement of the individual stories and which discarded a good deal of the framework material that was superfluous. *Mark, who basically does no more than arrange individual pericopes alongside each other, retains too much ancillary material that is not really productive even for the individual stories themselves.* The introductions to his pericopes still contain the ruins of an itinerary. Luke paid attention to these matters and sought to breathe life into them either by cutting or by expanding them. Matthew, by contrast, regarded all such things as secondary. *And since we have now irretrievably lost Jesus' actual itinerary, for which the Christian congregation from its beginnings had no interest, we have no choice, if we want to give some order to the Jesus stories, but to align ourselves with Matthew;* indeed, we shall at times have to go beyond him, for he often still clings too closely to Mark. For the most part, the Jesus stories all lie on the same plain. Only very occasionally are we able, by considering the internal character of a particular story, to give a somewhat more precise account of its chronological and geographical setting. But in general there is no life of Jesus in the sense of a developing narrative of his life, no chronological outline (*Aufriss*) of the story of Jesus; there are only individual stories, pericopes set within a framework (*Rahmenwerk*).[29]

It is worth pausing for a moment to consider the force and subsequent reception of such views about the chronology and topology of Mark's gospel. If the narrative outline of the gospel (a period of one year's activity, spent largely in Galilee, followed by a final visit to Jerusalem) is neither the result of historical reminiscence nor simply what was contained in the tradition, is it perhaps the deliberate and indeed theologically motivated creation of the evangelist himself? Schmidt allows that the overall framework (*Gesamtrahmen*) of the gospel— with its Galilean ministry, a section where Jesus moves out of Galilee into Gentile territory (6:14–8:26), and a final account of Jesus' activity and death in Jerusalem—is the work of the evangelist. On the other hand, he also shows that within each of these sections there is a great deal of confusion and that the topographical references are often only very loosely connected with those in previous section. Thus he writes of 6:14–8:26: "The complex as a whole is, as I have tried to show, composed of separate narrative units which were taken from the tradition available to the Evangelist. These individual pericopes contain much topographical and chronological material by way of framework (*Rahmenwerk*). Yet this is all simply set side by side without any artifice, so that these details can be viewed only as marking the breaks between the sections. The result is that, if one seeks to read the section as a continuous account with an itinerary, one is confronted with a topographical confusion which cannot be unscrambled."[30]

Nevertheless, a series of scholars have, since the time of Schmidt, argued that there is a discernible theological purpose behind Mark's topography.[31] This thesis is partly related to claims that Mark's views reflected the fact that there was, at the time he wrote, already an established Christian community in the areas that he ascribes to Galilee;[32] partly to the claim that Mark is making a central theological distinction between Galilee as a place of revelation and redemption, of eschatological fulfillment, and Jerusalem as the place of rejection.[33] The great stumbling block to this view is the clear evidence of Jesus' rejection: "Then Jesus said to them, 'Prophets are not without honor, except in their hometown, and among their own kin, and in their own house'" (6:4). Davies, who is sharply critical of this thesis, raises a question that is close to the heart of Schmidt's contention: "The question will insinuate itself whether the geographical references in the tradition, which, by much subtle exegesis, are made to yield the doctrinal interpretations proposed are not simply reminiscences or floating data, inaccurate or imprecise, preserved in the tradition, which do not necessarily demand those interpretations."[34] And he concludes his discussion of 6:1–6: "The rejection at Nazareth culminates the rejection of Jesus by his very own and points forward to his rejection by 'Israel.' Whatever view be taken of the place of 6:1–6 in the total structure of Mark, its importance for Mark is unmistakable. And it makes it impossible to think that Galilee for him was holy land."[35]

This is not to say that Mark has no design, no purpose in dividing Jesus' ministry as he does. The views raised by Lohmeyer and others do, in a sense, build on foundations laid by Schmidt. Even though he argued that the details of Mark's chronology and topography were largely the accidental result of the conjunction of existing material that had served a rather different purpose in the worship of the church, he still allowed that the *Gesamtrahmen* of the gospel was Mark's creation. This, in turn, leaves room for scholars to ask what purpose Mark might have had in thus constructing his narrative. The problem is that too often the answers given suppose that Mark has constructed a coherent story world that enshrines his theological views, whereas coherence is something extremely hard to find, not least in the detail of Mark's chronology and topography. Schmidt's work challenges all those who wish to investigate Mark's literary purposes to do so in a way that takes due note of the inconsistencies and contradictions in his account, which result precisely from his conjoining of traditional units of material with only minimal modification or adjustment. Mark works with the unadulterated, unrefined tradition. Whatever he does with it, whatever he makes of it (and this is not Schmidt's primary concern in *Der Rahmen*), he uses it straight, as it comes. This is Schmidt's primary insight, which arises from his painstaking examination of the details of Mark's chronology and topography. Only those who have grappled with the detail of such form-critical studies are in a position to attempt to set aside such claims. Anything else is, as Sir Isaiah Berlin is said to have remarked, an unprofitable exercise, like being sick before breakfast.[36]

It is this schooling in the character of what he calls, in the subtitle to his inquiry into the gospel framework, the earliest Jesus tradition, which forms the basis for Schmidt's major work on the nature and form of the Gospels, their literary character. In his article for the Gunkel *Festschrift,* his central thesis is that the gospels are part of folk-literature; they represent a kind of literary production that is closely tied to a particular *Sitz im Leben,* that of the collection of the sayings and stories of the activities of leading figures within a religious (or, in the case of the Faust legends, a quasi-religious) movement. Already we can see tendencies within them to develop in a more strictly literary manner; but as Franz Overbeck had clearly seen before him, there is a world of difference between patristic literature and the gospel writings.

Clearly, such a view of the gospels as *Kleinliteratur* is sharply differentiated from what has recently become a widely held view, namely, that the gospels are forms of Hellenistic biographies. Schmidt's discussion of this topic occurs in two sections of the present work: as part of his review of previous scholarship, and as a preliminary to his own substantive treatment of the topic. His treatment of earlier scholarship is largely critical, though he notes that the American Clyde Weber Votaw recognized the popular character of the gospels but was then more concerned with the comparison between the subjects of biographies (Socrates, Epictetus, Jesus) than with the nature of the particular forms. Again, he agrees with Heinrici that there is an important point of formal comparison between the gospels and memorabilia and biographies insofar as they both contain collections of material. It is not to be denied that ancient biographies are often not much more than a "patchwork of significant words and deeds of the hero" (4). Heinrici refers here to Diogenes Laertius as a prime example of someone who produces such loosely structured compilations of reminiscences and sources. Schmidt agrees that there are clear points of similarity here, but he wants clearly to distinguish the process whereby the two similarly loosely structured accounts came into being. While Diogenes Laertius's works are hastily thrown together collections of sources, poor examples of their genre indeed, the gospels are the result of "a natural process—not a laborious product but a lush growth." The complexity—and lack of coherence—is here the product of the development of a lively tradition within a cultic community rather than the result of hasty dictation! Diogenes Laertius claims to be an author, "writing a long foreword and naming his sources, and still manages to produce an incoherent work" (5). There is, that is to say, a radical difference between the kind of repetition, inconsistency, and variety of perspective that is to be found in the collected traditions of a young and rapidly developing religious community and the lack of coherence and inconsistency of an overhasty and overproductive ancient biographer juggling his many literary sources.

A further point needs to be picked up from this preliminary discussion. Johannes Weiss drew attention to the similarity between the modes of characterization in the gospels and in the peripatetic biographies, notably in Plutarch. What is distinctive here is the way that ἦθος is portrayed through πράξεις. But the point of contact is hardly sufficient to establish a generic link between the two forms. All sorts of popular literature, legends, and folk books describe the character of their heroes solely through their actions, but this clearly does not make them all peripatetic biographies. Again, there are similarities here that, according to Schmidt, have very different sources. Peripatetic biography is a conscious literary form that uses the device of indirect characterization: "the gospels, legends, and folk books developed through an unconscious process, which grew up all on its own" (12).

Schmidt returns to the topic briefly again in his own substantive treatment of the gospel genre, which is principally concerned with an exploration of analogies in popular forms of literature. Two points for him primarily distinguish the gospels from ancient biographies: the concern with portraiture in ancient biography, and the sense of the authorial personality. The Greek peripatetics were concerned to offer a portrait of their subjects through indirect characterization. Within the Alexandrian tradition of which Suetonius is an heir, greater stress is laid on the arrangement of material to give a rounded, coherent account of the subject's personality. Such portraits are offered for various purposes, not least as examples for the young to follow. But whatever the different styles and methods of portraiture, one thing that is clear is the conscious purpose and use of literary devices as evidenced in the authorial "I" which makes its presence felt throughout the work (see here earlier remarks, 6). The Synoptic Gospels have practically nothing of this. There is little interest in portraiture as such: one clear indication is the complete absence of any physical description of Jesus, whereas physical descriptions are a regular, if not indispensable, feature of ancient biographies. The authorial voice is almost entirely absent from Mark. It becomes much more audible in Luke, but then Luke's attempts to push the gospel form closer to more literary forms of writing have been carefully scrutinized by Schmidt in *Der Rahmen.* There are, indeed, those who would speak of biography even where there is no evidence of conscious literary purpose, but in this case it is better to forge a new term, *folk biography* (37).

It is precisely the difficulty of drawing the line between popular and more literary forms of biography that can lead to confusion. Schmidt is keenly aware of the overlaps that exist, just as he wants to fight vigorously for a recognition of the essentially popular character of the gospels. He knows that many ancient biographies were in fact modeled on the popular biography of Homer. Precisely, too, because of the use of oral tales and sayings, *chreiai,* in literary Lives, there are similarities with popular or folk books with their collection of oral material. Lucian's *Demonax,* with its long section of such anecdotes, clearly provides parallels to the gospels. More intriguingly, in Philostratus's *Apollonius of Tyana* it seems clear that the author has himself used collections of material as opposed simply to individual sayings and stories. In such a case, again, kinds of inconsistency very similar to those found in the gospels will be produced precisely because here material very similar in kind to that of the gospels is imported into the narrative. For all that, Philostratus's work remains that of a self-conscious literary writer who comments on his sources and on his subject. How different ultimately from the gospels, with their absence of any kind of periodization or psychologization!

All this is but a preliminary to the present work, whose main focus is on such analogies to the gospels as may be found in the history of literature, specifically within the field of collections of folktales and sayings. Schmidt's point is that we must seek analogies rather than genealogies to the gospels, casting the net as widely as possible to find texts that reflect a similar *Sitz im Leben.* Specifically, what he is looking for are texts in which the deeds and sayings of central or innovative religious figures (including Dr. Faustus under this head) have been collected more or less directly from the oral tradition. Thus, *The Sayings of the Fathers (Apophthegmata Patrum)* provides an interesting analogy because it contains the sayings of the desert saints as they were recorded by those who visited the desert monasteries and brought them back. In such a situation, there is a strong impulse to preserve the tradition,[37] although this process of preservation is complex and associated with a wealth of textual variants.[38] A number of scholars had already drawn attention to the importance of such material: Wilhelm Bousset with his study of the *Apophthegmata Patrum,* and Wilhelm Michaelis and B. H. Streeter with studies of the Sadhu tradition. The general direction of such studies had been pointed to in Paul Wendland's *Die urchristlichen Literaturformen.* What is particularly illuminating is Wendland's recognition of the tension that is involved in such a process between creativity and faithfulness to the tradition: "Artistic creativity and unity is constrained by dependence on traditional material" (quoted p. 20).

It is not my intention to rehearse the detail of Schmidt's arguments in this present work, but rather to set it in the wider context both of his own earlier form-critical studies and of other contemporary debate, as well as to address the question of its reception. The main section of "The Place of the Gospels" is dedicated to a detailed comparison between the gospels and various examples of "oral literature"—works, that is to say, that have very close connections with oral tradition. Chief among these studies is his extended analysis of the Faust legends and their various recensions. Here, I think, it is appropriate to draw out two points that will be of importance for the concluding section of this essay, where I wish to return to more recent attempts to classify the gospels as ancient biographies, which have in many ways misread and misrepresented Schmidt's views.

First, Schmidt points out that the many versions of the Faust legends betray a pattern of literary relationships similar to that of the Synoptic Gospels. Of the earliest of these versions, Spiess's betrays many of the characteristics of the Synoptics: doublets and contradictions occur as there; above all, the seams between the different stories are all too apparent, and Spiess has been roundly criticized for his lack of literary ability. But as Schmidt points out, "The perspective is all wrong: writers of folk books are not so much authors as they are mere collectors and spokesmen for a tradition that has been carried along by a people" (58–59). The second point relates more to the subsequent redactions of Spiess's version, which attempted to smooth over some of the cracks and to produce a greater agreement in the details of chronology and topography. Schmidt asks why such changes occurred and observes that a few things at least can be said clearly about the tendencies of individual editions. "Since Widman says that Faust studied in Ingolstadt rather than in Wittenberg, obviously this sinful man of the world must have been a Catholic, and Pfitzer's clever calculations prove that the whole story took place in the time 'before Luther's blessed Reformation,' when the ancient papal system was in full swing. Such views are based on a general impression given by the oldest Faust book, for it has long been noted that the earliest compiler betrays a decidedly Protestant tendency . . ." (49). We need, that is, to recognize that such collections are by no means innocent: they give expression to deeply held beliefs and prejudices, which can be documented in often minor redactional changes. At the same time, such evidence of tendencies within the collections is not to be equated with the kind of artistic creativity that is displayed in consciously literary works with their much greater authorial presence and their greater freedom in the arrangement and interpretation of the material itself.

At this point let us return to the criticisms leveled against the form critics that we noted above and consider their relevance specifically to Schmidt's work. These were (1) that the form critics made too sharp and absolute a distinction between *Hoch-* and *Kleinliteratur,* with the result that they were unwilling to ask questions about the genre of the gospels;[39] or (2) to consider any kind of analogy with the gospels (the latter point specifically against Bultmann); (3) that such an approach led to the eclipse of the author and excluded any consideration of the evangelists' intention or purpose; and (4) that the form-critical view emphasized the unique character of the gospels.

One of the problems about this blanket treatment of the form critics' views is that it blurs certain important disagreements between Schmidt and Bultmann. These can be most clearly documented in the concluding pages of *Die Geschichte der synoptischen Tradition,* to which Burridge refers.[40] There Bultmann quite explicitly distances himself from Schmidt, agreeing with Schmidt that folk collections (*volkstümliche Sammlungen*) share certain characteristics with the gospels, while insisting, nonetheless, that they differ in that "they do not tell of an admired human personality but of the Son of God, Jesus Christ, the Lord of the congregation, in that they have developed out of the Christ-cult and remain linked to it."[41]

This conflation accounts, I assume, for the surprising charge against Schmidt that he refuses to look for analogies (of any kind) for the gospels, whereas this is clearly the central intention of "The Place of the Gospels." Not only does he look for them (as, indeed, does Bultmann), but he is convinced that he has found them in the popular collections of the *Apophtegmata Patrum* and in the Francis and the Faust legends. There is, moreover, a further confusion that creeps into Burridge's treatment of Bultmann, which concerns the extent to which Bultmann addresses the question of the genre of the gospels at all. Here Bultmann's views are similar to those of Schmidt. It is not the case that Bultmann concludes "that we cannot even talk in terms of genre for the gospels."[42] What Bultmann argues is that the gospels are not *literary* forms—not, that is, the product of a developed set of literary conventions, ones, moreover, that are consciously developed and discussed by the author. They are, according to Bultmann, expanded "cult-legends."[43] And *legend* is a generic term. But it is true that Bultmann adds, rather confusingly, that they are sui generis, that they constitute a new genre, distinct from all others. It is at this point that Schmidt and Bultmann differ.

With these preliminaries, we can now turn to the heart of the matter, which lies with the twofold charge that Schmidt makes a far too rigid distinction between *Hoch-* and *Kleinliteratur* and that he fails to do justice to the authorial activities of the evangelists.

Schmidt certainly wants to make a sharp distinction in principle between conscious literary works that are the product of developed literary traditions and conventions, and works that are first and foremost literary records of oral material. In practice, he recognizes that there are literary works that consciously observe the literary conventions but contain collections of oral material, so that they overlap at many points with more popular works (*Volksbücher*), such as Philostratus's *Life of Apollonius of Tyana* and Lucian's *Demonax;* just as there are popular works that are in a measure recast in the manner of more literary creations, such as Luke's gospel, which claims to give a coherent account of things but yet retains many of the inconsistencies of Mark's topography and chronology. The form critics, as the present work with its introductory survey of earlier scholarship makes clear, were perfectly well aware of the connections between Greco-Roman biography and more popular forms of literature. Nevertheless, they were right, I judge, to want to make a clear distinction. And the difference for them lay crucially in the role of the author.

Here Bultmann and Schmidt were in agreement. Certainly characteristics of ancient biographies (perhaps not present in every case, but constituting a cluster of family resemblances of which at least a number are always to be found) were typically lacking in the gospels. Such characteristics were, according to Bultmann, "the lack of any scientific character, and developed techniques of composition, of any interest in chronology, in making substantive connections between the individual units, and in psychological motivation."[44] Schmidt would have added the lack of any interest in itineraries and topography, and would perhaps have qualified Bultmann's point about substantive connections, pointing out that collectors of traditions would group these according to certain topics even if the nature of these topics might sometimes be rather obscure. Above all, as we have seen, he would have wanted to stress the lack of interest in portraiture.[45]

It may be that Schmidt offers less overt methodological reflection on the nature of literary genres and the proper manner of their definition than do some recent discussions; for all that, there is a good deal of perceptive comment here that adds up to more than just a simple view of the matter. It is certainly right, as has recently been argued, to regard genre as constituted by a range of characteristics, both formal and material (relating to matters of content), with flexible and fluid boundaries, and to see genres as having their place within sets of literary relationships between different genres. But nothing in the above differentiation of popular folk collections from ancient biography offends against such canons; indeed, it can easily be construed in such terms. What such a view of genre does is to alert one to the inevitability of boundary disputes and to the need for great care in adjudicating them. Here, it seems to me, there is much to be learned from the admittedly rather cursory remarks of Schmidt in the present essay.

Let us consider two cases, Lucian's *Demonax* and Philostratus's *Apollonius of Tyana.* Lucian's work, which is entitled *The Life of Demonax,* is of simple structure. It contains an opening section that, after setting out the author's reasons for writing (that "young men of good instincts . . . may be able to set themselves a pattern from our modern world," 2), gives a brief outline of Demonax's origins, character, and career, followed by a central section consisting of a catenae of his sayings, introduced simply by "I should like to cite a few of his well-directed and witty remarks" (12). The book concludes with a brief account of his death and a final remark, strongly reminiscent of the conclusion of the Fourth Gospel: "These are a very few things out of many which I might have mentioned, but they will suffice to give my readers a notion of the sort of man he was" (67).

As Hubert Cancik has remarked, the form of this treatise is a mixture of βίος and teaching (διδαχή, δόγμα).[46] This is appropriate for a philosopher whose teaching was not that of the lecture theater but of reflection on everyday life. The treatise has, according to Cancik, a very definite purpose, which is to promote a certain kind of Hellenism; it is anti-Roman and strongly pro-Athenian. Thus, *Demonax* appears as a clearly if simply structured work with a clear purpose and line of argument and with a distinct authorial voice. Lucian tells us what he is about and why, and presents his picture of Demonax with clarity and authority.

There are also features of the text that remind us of the kind of presentation of Jesus' teaching that we find in the gospels. The central section is a series of briefly recounted sayings and exchanges that highlight Demonax's attitudes and beliefs and that exhibit his wit and sharpness of mind. The individual units are loosely connected; in some cases they are linked by topic or by persons, in others they are contrasted. The setting is for the most part Athens; only at the end is there a transition to Olympia. It is clear that there is considerable similarity between collections of sayings such as these and those to be found in the gospels. Dibelius, as Schmidt indicates (23f.) drew attention to this in his *Die Formgeschichte des Evangeliums*. Distinguishing between the matter of the Greek *chreiai* to be found in *Demonax* and the *chreiai* associated with Jesus, Dibelius nevertheless stressed the similarity of form and explained this by reference to their unliterary origin.[47] They would have been preserved, he thinks, in the first place as individual pieces in circles closely associated with the "hero," then more widely. Only gradually would they have been taken up into larger complexes, where their individuality might be clearly preserved or else where they were developed in a more literary manner.[48] The fact, however, that there are formal similarities between sections of *Demonax* and of Mark does not imply that as works they therefore belong to the same genre. It is simply that they both draw on similar material. Nevertheless, the manner of presentation of the material as a whole is quite distinctive, as the framing sections of *Demonax* make clear. Here the authorial personality is clearly to the fore, and the literary methods and moral purpose of the work are clearly enunciated. Mark's opening, by contrast, draws immediately on traditional material, without any account of his manner or purpose in doing so. What he does is to summon up the traditions of Isaiah to provide a setting for his narrative in sacred history and geography.

In Philostratus's *Life of Apollonius of Tyana,* there is, as was noted by Dibelius,[49] a considerable difference in the character of the stories told about Apollonius from those in Lucian's *Demonax*. The *chreiai* are more developed,[50] and we encounter more extensive complexes of material.[51] The elaborated form of the stories already distances them significantly from the gospels and suggests that there has been substantial development either by Philostratus or during the period of collection and retelling. But on the other hand, the loose way in which the stories are collected and the lack of detailed concern with chronology suggest that Philostratus is indeed working with complexes of material that have already loosely connected individual stories. The real similarity with the gospels is thus between the traditions that are used; the greatest divergence lies in the literary voice of the authors. We are conscious all the time of Philostratus commenting and presenting his tale; whereas Mark, for all that he is a storyteller of great power, is presenting the tradition, not sorting through it, commenting on it and his sources.

That is to say, it is above all in the different attitude (explicit and implicit) to their sources that the distinctiveness of the evangelists and the ancient biographers is most apparent. Clearly both evangelists and biographers use sources, but there is a sense of critical distance in the ancient biographers that is almost entirely absent in the evangelists.[52] The biographers have a much greater freedom to present their material according to their own lights, whereas the evangelists, for all that they may shade and nuance their material, are essentially bound to the tradition.[53] Whatever else the evangelists were, they were not ancient biographers, even if in compiling and presenting the traditions of Jesus' deeds and sayings, of his life and death, they were inevitably inviting comparison with ancient biographies.

In what way, then, may we characterize the literary work of the evangelists? Schmidt's insistence on the sense in which the gospels are vehicles through which the tradition comes to expression, in which the tradition is still living (as witness their richness), poses an insuperable obstacle to those who see the work of the redaction critics as justifying a simple equation between the creativity of the evangelists and that of ancient biographers.[54] On the other hand, Schmidt does not altogether deny that the evangelists and other collectors of folk traditions may have their own intentions and purposes in producing such collections. As we have seen, the collections of Faust legends may well have Protestant theological tendencies. Even though it is a characteristic of much of this literature to take over topographical settings of individual units with a cheerful disregard for their coherence within the larger literary complex, this does not mean that such collectors may not use topography as a means of making a theological point. Setting the Faust stories in Ingolstadt may be a none too subtle way of making an anti-Catholic point.

But it would be useless to pretend that Schmidt's contribution to this topic is particularly far-reaching, useful though it is as a start. Here we can do no more than attempt to spell out some of the issues that his work raises and point in the most general terms to ways in which they might be addressed.

In the first place, we should guard against assuming that the tradition is, as it were, neutral, and that the evangelists have unlimited freedom to impose theological meaning on it. The form critics, Bultmann to the fore, were fully alert to the possibility of there being theological tendencies that shaped the tradition. Bultmann looked for certain kinds of mythologizing tendencies that accentuated the christological motifs within the tradition and believed that he could discern a relatively uniform process of traditioning that promoted a particular form of cosmology/worldview. (Against such tendencies, a creative theologian like the

Fourth Evangelist could indeed protest and act by a form of existential interpretation of the myth, which in his case had assumed gnostic colors.) There is, however, no compelling reason to suppose that the theological tendencies of the synoptic tradition were largely uniform and coherent. All that we otherwise know of the early Christian church would make this surprising, to say the least. If this is true,[55] then we have to assume that the evangelists are working with traditional material that contains diverse and possibly conflicting theological tendencies, which promote, that is to say, different and even fundamentally opposed views of the world.

Thus, an evangelist like Mark is working with materials that have diverse tendencies and trying to shape and steer them in a particular direction. He does this not by setting them within a discursive, reflective framework that presents a philosophical or moral view of the hero and so provides a coherent setting for stories that may indeed be taken from the tradition; rather, he makes his point by weaving together material of diverse kinds to create what Ernest Best has appropriately described as a collage.[56] In a collage, materials which originally had quite other purposes (pieces of newsprint, patches of material, etc.) are brought together to form a new aesthetic object. Similarly, here different units of material from the oral traditions about Jesus, from written collections of such materials, from Hebrew scripture, and from contemporary apocalyptic and proverbial circles are brought together to form a whole that makes a complex statement of its own. The analogy will take us only so far. In a way it suggests that there is a greater tension between original use and setting than is perhaps the case with the gospels, but it may encourage us to look more carefully to see the fault lines and to discern the different tendencies that the material contains.

To revert to the subject that occupied Schmidt so greatly in *Der Rahmen:* the topography of Mark's gospel is in many ways chaotic. It is possible only with a great deal of effort to make sense of Jesus' itinerary in chapters 6–8. While Mark clearly structures his gospel into a Galilean and a Jerusalem period, it is not at all easy to discern what, if any, the underlying tendency of this move might be. The more we press the details of the individual units within the two sections, the less coherence we find. There is rejection in Galilee as well as in Jerusalem; there is revelation in Jerusalem as well as in Galilee. This should not deter us from any attempt to find a tendency or tendencies in this division. I have proposed elsewhere,[57] following in part suggestions from Elisabeth Struthers Malbon,[58] that there is a division between traditional notions of sacred space centered on the temple, which are essentially static, and a view of sacred space that is dynamic and that takes Jesus' itinerant Galilean ministry as paradigmatic for the life of the Christian congregation. The presence of God, which was associated with the temple on Mount Zion and which was to be restored on the return of the exiles along the way of the Lord as was announced at the beginning of Mark's gospel, is to be found wherever the gospel is preached (13:10). It is not, that is to say, that Galilee is substituted as the new holy land (*terra christiana*) for the sacred places of Jerusalem; it is rather that Galilee becomes the figure for a new mode of sacred geography, where God's presence is realized wherever his followers obey his call and mission.

Such major shifts in cosmology/worldview are not achieved by providing an explanatory framework of an explicit kind and then filling it out with collections of traditional material, as in the case of Lucian's *Demonax*. Rather, Mark works more by simple process of juxtaposition. Scriptural motifs, such as the Isaianic theme of the return of the exiles along the way of the Lord, are set alongside narrative material about Jesus' itinerant ministry and call of the disciples, his final journey to Jerusalem, his death outside the city and the rending of the temple veil, and the story of the message to the disciples to go to Galilee in such a way that as the reader/hearer follows the lines of the narrative, his or her understanding of these motifs is gradually recast. Such a process will inevitably throw up many inconsistencies and contradictions. Some of these will be of a relatively trivial kind of the sort noticed by Schmidt in his *Der Rahmen*. Others will lie at a deeper level: precisely because the diverse material used has its own theological tendencies, we must expect to find deep-seated theological oppositions too. The notion of the way of the Lord is closely associated with the idea that Israel's ills are the result of its disobedience to God for which it has been punished by exile. Repentance and renewed obedience will lead to return to the promised land and the restoration of the former glory. On the other hand, there are other motifs, associated not least with the stories of the exorcisms, which suggest that humanity's plight has its roots in a demonic invasion of the world from which only a divine intervention can save it. The scene of the action shifts, as it were, from a concern with the restoration of Zion to concern with the purging of the whole world from demonic infestation. It is not enough, simply, that God should be in his temple protecting Israel from the incursions of the nations: God's presence is required wherever his followers do battle with the powers of evil, whether these are in demonic spirits or in the hearts and minds of men and women. This juxtaposition of material with very different theological tendencies gives the gospel much of its internal tension and dynamic and cannot be explored further here. Suffice it to say that this way of attempting to construe the editorial activity of the evangelists does justice to the hard-won insights of the form critics' detailed studies of the synoptic tradition, while extending the notion of the evangelists' theological intentions.

I began by saying that Schmidt's work has been largely neglected by English-speaking scholars. The present work will, I hope, encourage a closer look at the work of one of the major figures of twentieth-century literary critical studies of the gospels. It should help to correct some of the half-truths that have come to be accepted about the work both of the form critics and the redaction critics, and it should serve to reopen the debate about the literary genre of the gospels. It is a long overdue tribute to a fine scholar whose academic integrity and originality was matched by his political courage and will.

NOTES

1. Wrede, *Das Messiasgeheimnis in den Evangelien: Zugleich ein Beitrag zum Verständnis des Markusevangeliums* (Göttingen: Vandenhoeck & Ruprecht, 1901); translated as *The Messianic Secret* (Cambridge: James Clarke, 1971).

2. Bultmann, *Die Geschichte der synoptischen Tradition* (Göttingen: Vandenhoeck & Ruprecht, 1921; translated as *The History of the Synoptic Tradition* [Oxford: Basil Blackwell, 1961]). Martin Dibelius, *Die Formgeschichte des Evangeliums* (Tübingen: J. C. B. Mohr [Paul Siebeck], 1919), fared somewhat better. Its English translation appeared as *From Tradition to Gospel* (London: Ivor Nicholson and Watson), in 1934.

3. Schmidt, *Der Rahmen der Geschichte Jesu: Literarkritische Untersuchungen zur ältesten Jesusüberlieferung* (Berlin: Trowitzsch & Sohn, 1919).

4. B. H. Streeter, *The Four Gospels: A Study of Origins Treating of the Manuscript Traditions, Sources, Authorship, and Dates* (London: Macmillan, 1924).

5. Cf. A. von Harnack, *What is Christianity?* (Philadelphia: Fortress, 1986): "In the first place, they [the first three Gospels] offer us a plain picture of Jesus' teaching, in regard both to its main features and to its individual application; in the second place, they tell us how his life issued in the service of his vocation; and in the third place, they describe to us the impression which he made upon his disciples, and which they transmitted" (31). For Harnack the authority of Matthew and Luke was based on their faithful transmission of Mark and Q. See too, F. C. Burkitt's intriguing defense of Mark's apocalyptic presentation of Jesus in *The Earliest Sources for the Life of Jesus* (London: Constable, 1922): "And therefore the Gospel of Mark, which makes so much of transcendental hopes and claims, which bases so much on the personal ascendency of Jesus, is more likely to reflect the historical truth than any view which regards the mission of Jesus as 'purely religio-ethical and humanitarian'" (72).

6. On this point, as Schweitzer noted in *The Quest for the Historical Jesus: A Critical Study of Its Progress from Reimarus to Wrede* (London: A. & C. Black, 1936), Wrede's views are carefully nuanced. It is not possible that Mark should have invented such an idea. Nevertheless, this is "not to deny that Mark has a share and perhaps a considerable share in the creation of the view which he sets forth" (337–38). Wrede's work has rightly been claimed as a forerunner of the work of the redaction-critics. But, for all that, it certainly sheds light on the editorial role of the evangelists and promotes further study of their shaping of the tradition, it is primarily a work of historical enquiry into the life of Jesus. Stripping away the theological tendencies of the gospels can bring us closer to the real, historical Jesus. The trouble with this, as Sanday protested, was that it stripped away elements of the Gospel which appeared to support belief in Jesus' messianic self-consciousness.

7. Sanday, *The Life of Christ in Recent Research* (Oxford: Clarendon Press, 1907).

8. Ibid., 71.

9. The nationalistic tones of Sanday's attack verge on the racist: "He writes in the style of a Prussian official. He has all the arrogance of a certain kind of common sense. His mind is mathematical, with something of the stiffness of mathematics—a mind of the type which is supposed to ask of everything, What does it prove?" (70).

10. *The Immortals: The Spiritual Heroes of Humanity, Their Life and Work*. Cf. Thomas Carlyle, *On Heroes and Hero-Worship and the Heroic in History* (London: Chapman and Hall, 1872).

11. *Religion in Geschichte und Gegenwart,* 2d ed., vol. 3 (1929), 110–51.

12. In a manner not far removed from Geza Vermes's most recent account of Jesus in *The Religion of Jesus the Jew* (London: SCM Press, 1993), see my review in *Journal of Theological Studies* 47 (1996): 201–8.

13. Cf. his letter to Barth of 10 December 1926, in *Karl Barth–Rudolf Bultmann Briefwechsel, 1922–66,* ed. Bernd Jaspert, *Karl Barth Gesamtausgabe, V. Briefe,* vol. 1 (Zurich: Theologischer Verlag Zurich, 1971), where he presents his Jesus book as dealing with the question of the relation of John to the Synoptics or as the question "how we are to understand (of course not to explain causally) the fact that the proclaimer Jesus becomes Jesus Christ who is proclaimed (*"wie aus dem Verkündiger Jesus der Verkündigte Jesus Christus wird"*) (63–65). See too the much later debate with Ernst Käsemann and others over the New Quest for the historical Jesus and Bultmann's *Das Verhältnis der urchristlichen Christusbotschaft zum historischen Jesus,* Sitzungsberichte der Heidelberger Akademie der Wissenschaften, Philosophisch-historische Klasse, Jg. 1960, Abhandlung no. 3 (Heidelberg: Carl Winter, Universitätsverlag, 1962).

14. One of the earliest of these is Vincent Taylor's *The Formation of the Gospel Tradition* (London: Macmillan, 1933). While referring briefly to Schmidt's *Eucharisterion* article, he does not mention *Der Rahmen* at all; in general he focuses much more on Bultmann's *Geschichte der synoptischen Tradition,* to which he gives a cautious welcome.

15. Dodd, *Parables of the Kingdom* (London: Nisbet, 1935). Dodd, however, did not accept Schmidt's arguments about the framework of the gospel narratives and argued instead that the Markan framework represented a "genuine succession of events," *ET* 43 (1932): 400.

16. Dodd's *The Founder of Christianity* (London: Collins, 1971) won the Collins prize. His views were taken up and developed by Joachim Jeremias, whose *Parables of Jesus* (London: SCM, 1963) enjoyed a similar popularity.

17. See, for example, Morna Hooker's *The Message of Mark* (London: Epworth, 1983) and her remark: "It will not, I hope, be regarded as a sexist remark if I suggest that only a man could have used the phrase "like pearls on a string" to suggest a haphazard arrangement of material. Any woman would have spotted at once the flaw in the analogy: pearls need to be carefully selected and graded. And gradually it has dawned on New Testament scholars that this is precisely what the evangelists have done with their material" (2–3). The point is well taken; but the inappropriateness of the analogy to Schmidt's point is one thing; the claim that while "[t]he stories may not be in order chronologically," "they most certainly have an order" (3) is what needs to be tested. See too, Hooker, *The Gospel according to St. Mark* (London: A. & C. Black, 1991). Here Hooker notes that though "the extreme scepticism of certain form-critics" (could she not bell the cat?) "led many scholars (especially outside Germany) to reject their views, their contribution to Markan studies has ultimately proved enormous." (10) This is a less than wholly gracious recognition of the form critics' achievement; a fuller acknowledgment that English-speaking gospel-scholarship hobbled itself by failing to pay adequate attention to the work of the form critics would have been in order.

18. Nineham, *St. Mark,* Pelican New Testament Commentaries (Harmondsworth: Penguin, 1963).

19. Best, *Following Jesus: Discipleship in the Gospel of Mark,* JSNTSup 4 (Sheffield: JSOT, 1981); Best, *Disciples and Discipleship: Studies in the Gospel according to Mark* (Edinburgh: T. & T. Clark, 1986).

20. An excellent balancing of these two concerns is to be found in John Drury's rather neglected *Tradition and Design in Luke's Gospel: A Study in Early Christian Historiography* (London: Darton, Longman and Todd, 1976). See, too, G. Stanton's comments in *A Gospel for a New People: Studies in Matthew* (Edinburgh: T. & T. Clark, 1992), 23–53.

21. Burridge, *What Are the Gospels? A Comparison with Graeco-Roman Biography*, Society for New Testament Studies Monograph Series 70 (Cambridge: Cambridge University Press, 1992).

22. Ibid., 11.

23. Ibid., 12.

24. Ibid.

25. Ibid.

26. Schmidt, *Der Rahmen der Geschichte Jesu: Literarkritische Untersuchungen zur ältesten Jesusüberlieferung* (Berlin: Trowitzsch & Sohn, 1919).

27. Augustine, *De consensu evangelistarum,* 2.21.51f. The influence of such views was, according to Schmidt, extensive: "Das ganze Mittelalter war von dem Gedanken beherrscht, daß kein Evangelist in chronologischer Reihenfolge geschrieben habe (The whole of the Middle Ages was dominated by the idea that no evangelist had written his Gospel in chronological order)" (*Der Rahmen,* 10).

28. "Stories relating to the history of Jesus in the first period went from mouth to mouth. When Christians were together, they told each other stories about the Lord's sayings and deeds, taking over from each other, complementing each other. . . . One story freely followed another in this oral exchange. When one person finished, another continued 'and it happened that. . .'" (*Der Rahmen,* 19).

29. *Der Rahmen*, 317, italics mine.

30. Ibid., 208–9.

31. The most important of these are E. Lohmeyer, *Galiäa und Jerusalem,* Forschungen zur Religion und Literatur des Alten und Neuen Testaments (Gottingen: Vandenhoeck & Ruprecht, 1936); R. H. Lightfoot, *Locality and Doctrine in the Gospels* (London, Hodder & Stoughton: 1938); W. Marxsen, *Der Evangelist Markus: Studien zur Redaktionsgeschichte des Evangeliums*, Forschungen zur Religion und Literatur des Alten und Neuen Testaments (Göttingen: Vandenhoeck & Ruprecht, 1956); S. Freyne, *Galilee, Jesus, and the Gospels: Literary Approaches and Historical Investigations* (Philadelphia: Fortress Press, 1988). For a full discussion of the literature see G. Stemberger, "Galilee—Land of Salvation?" in *The Gospel and the Land: Early Christianity and Jewish Territorial Doctrine,* ed. W. D. Davies, The Biblical Seminar 25 (Sheffield: JSOT Press, 1994), app. 4, 409–38.

32. This is particularly argued by Lohmeyer and Marxsen, who see Galilee as a *terra christiana,* where the church was already established. For details, see Stemberger, "Galilee—Land of Salvation?" 411–14, though they differ over the precise history of the establishment of the church in Galilee.

33. These views are broadly shared by Lohmeyer, Lightfoot, and Freyne.

34. Davies, *The Gospel and the Land,* 221–22.

35. Ibid., 239.

36. He was referring to logical positivists' rejection, without appropriate study, of metaphysics.

37. Cf. Ernest Best's important article "Mark's Preservation of the Tradition," in *The Interpretation of Mark,* ed. W. Telford (London: SPCK, 1974), 119–33, which shows how Mark retains material which is theologically unattractive to him.

38. See Hans Lietzmann's comments on Anthony's *Life of Simeon Stylites*, quoted on pp. 28–29.

39. See too the remarks in Burridge, *What Are the Gospels?*: "On this basis, questions may well be asked about the form of the individual units, but not the genre of the gospel as a whole" (8–9).

40. Burridge refers to the English translation (Oxford: Blackwell, 1963), which is made from the third revised edition of the German text (Gottingen: Vandenhoeck & Ruprecht, 1957) (*What Are the Gospels?*, 9–11). This translation contains the references to Schmidt's present essay, written after the first edition of Bultmann's work.

41. Bultmann, *Geschichte*, 398, my translation.

42. Burridge, *What Are the Gospels?*, 11.

43. Bultmann, *Geschichte*, 396, "erweiterte Kultuslegenden," cited by Burridge, *What Are the Gospels?*, 10.

44. Bultmann, *Geschichte*, 398.

45. In this sense he might have been somewhat puzzled by Bultmann's stated ground for rejecting his proposed analogy with folk collection, namely that they tell of "einer bewunderten menschlichen Persönlichkeit" (an admired human personality) by contrast with the Gospels which tell of the Son of God, Jesus Christ" (*Geschichte*, 398). Schmidt's view was that such collections were concerned with the words and deeds of the particular religious figure/s on whom the cult centered, not with the portrayal of their personality.

46. H. Cancik, "Bios und Logos: Formengeschichtliche Untersuchungen zu Lukians "Leben des Demonax," in *Markus-Philologie: Historische, literargeschichtliche und stilistische Untersuchungen zum zweiten Evangelium*, ed. H. Cancik (Tübingen: J. C. B. Mohr [Paul Siebeck], 1984), 115–30.

47. "Die als Schüler—bei den Griechen vielleicht als Gegner—an den "Helden" interessierten Kreise bewahren Äußerungen und Vorgänge auf, um Gesinnung und Weisung des Helden als maßgebende Norm (im Falle der Gegner: als typisches Gegenbeispiel) festzuhalten." M. Dibelius, *Die Formgeschichte des Evangeliums* (Tübingen: J. C. B. Mohr [Paul Siebeck], 1933), 156.

48. Dibelius cites *Demonax* as an example of the former, *Apollonius of Tyana* as an example of the latter, 152–53.

49. See n. 36 above.

50. Cf. B. L. Mack, "Elaboration of the Chreia in the Hellenistic School," in *Patterns of Persuasion in the Gospels,* ed. B. L. Mack and V. K. Robbins (Sonoma, Calif.: Polebridge Press, 1989), who points to the rhetorical exercises prescribed in the handbooks, in which students had to develop simple chreiai according to various principles (31–67).

51. There has been much discussion of the question of the fictitious nature of Philostratus's sources. Eduard Meyer (see Schmidt's discussion, 41–42) argued that "P. invented his written sources as part of a latent polemic against Moiragenes." Others have disputed this. Schmidt in the present work believes that it has to be assumed that "Damis" and the other pieces already had a history behind them, going back to traditions close to the historical Apollonius. It is strange that Burridge regards these debates as "too complex a distraction to our task to go into here," 160 (see useful n. 18): if Philostratus invented his sources, then he was a very different kind of writer indeed from the Synoptic Evangelists.

52. The exception suggested by Luke's prologue is more apparent than real when we come to consider Luke's actual use of his sources, where his redaction is often largely cosmetic and often none too skillful.

53. *Pace* Burridge, "Redaction criticism has freed us from seeing the evangelists as mere slaves of the oral tradition: instead, they are creative theologians and literary artists who took their source material and turned it into the gospel according to their understanding . . . *Thus the freedom to select and edit sources to produce the desired picture of the subject is another feature shared by both the gospels and Graeco-Roman* βίοι" (*What Are the Gospels?*, 204–5).

54. One should not assume that the work of the redaction critics is itself without significant challengers. Those who wish to see Mark as a literary artist creating his own coherent story world with its own coherent theology have first to answer the penetrating criticisms of Heikki Raisanen's *The "Messianic Secret" in Mark* (Edinburgh: T. & T. Clark, 1990).

55. A vivid example of conflicting theological tendencies is to be found in the Beelzebul controversy, Mark 3:20–30 pars. The contradiction between the senses of the two parabolic sayings which are contained in Jesus' reply was noticed by C. F. Evans, *Saint Luke*, New Testament Commentaries (London: SCM Press, 1990), 491, and is the subject of detailed treatment by J. Marcus, "The Beelzebul Controversy and the Eschatologies of Jesus," in *Authenticating the Activities of Jesus,* ed. Bruce D. Chilton and Craig A. Evans (Leiden: Brill, 1999), 247–77. The "Kingdom divided" assumes that Satan's kingdom is intact and active; the "Strong Man Bound" asserts that he has been overpowered: two very different cosmologies.

56. Ernest Best, "Mark's Preservation of the Tradition," in *The Interpretation of Mark,* ed. W. Telford (London: SPCK, 1985, 128).

57. John Riches, *Conflicting Mythologies: Identity Formation in the Gospels of Mark and Matthew* (Edinburgh: T. & T. Clark, 2000).

58. Malbon, *Narrative Space and Mythic Meaning in Mark's Gospel* (Sheffield: Sheffield Academic Press, 1991).

TRANSLATOR'S INTRODUCTION

As a leading exponent of the form-critical *(formgeschichtlich)* method, Karl Ludwig Schmidt was one of three German scholars whose work profoundly reshaped the field of New Testament studies during the early twentieth century. Along with Rudolf Bultmann's *History of the Synoptic Tradition* and Martin Dibelius's *From Tradition to Gospel*, K. L. Schmidt's writings (particularly *Die Stellung der Evangelien in der allgemeinen Literaturgeschichte*, which appeared in 1923, and *Der Rahmen der Geschichte Jesu*, published in 1919) helped introduce New Testament scholars to a new and provocative set of techniques for studying the biblical text. Form criticism, which had previously been applied to the Hebrew Bible by Hermann Gunkel, went on to have a lasting and substantial impact on literary and historical analysis of the New Testament. Among Schmidt's most important contributions was his argument, laid out in *Die Stellung*, that form criticism entailed an entirely new approach to the problem of the genre of the gospels. John Riches' essay in this volume traces the wide extent and enduring importance of Schmidt's assertion that the gospels are not comparable to any biographical literature from antiquity, but rather to oral literature from many different regions and periods.

Despite this contribution to our discipline, however, today K. L. Schmidt is not nearly as well known as Bultmann and Dibelius, at least in the English-speaking world. His relative obscurity is due in part to the fact that, unlike his more famous contemporaries, Schmidt has never been translated into English, so that he has become (like Josephus, perhaps) one of those writers whose work is cited more often than it is actually read. The present volume is the first installment in an effort to redress this unfortunate situation and to make the monographs of K. L. Schmidt more readily available to English-speaking students of the New Testament.

The strength and originality of Schmidt's ideas in *Die Stellung* were unfortunately not matched by equal clarity in his German prose. On the contrary, Schmidt couched the seminal insights of this monograph in a German style that can be fairly described as affected, wordy, convoluted, and bombastic. At times the text is so oblique as to become evasive. Schmidt coins new terms (*Schriftstellerpersönlichkeit*, for example), uses others in unusual senses (the Gospels, for example, were *spröde* against literary development), and then combines these words into sentences that at times become virtually trackless. At one point in the work of translating this monograph, for example, I was befuddled by a tangled sentence near the beginning of Part Two. After trying unsuccessfully for several hours to unlock its secrets, I took the text to my colleague, Prof. Erika

Scavillo, a native speaker of German. After a few minutes of careful scrutiny, with furrowed brow and repeated muttering, she finally exclaimed, "Ah, so that's what it says! Yes, now I see it. But nobody writes that way anymore."

Schmidt's motives for expressing himself in such a forbidding way belong to the history and sociology of German biblical scholarship, and I will not pursue them here. But the nature of his text poses a problem for the work of translation, not only because it is occasionally hard to determine exactly what he meant to say, but also because it is often difficult to render his German prose in clear English. It would be relatively easy to translate Schmidt's daunting German into opaque English, but what would be the point of that? His arguments are broad-minded, creative, and intelligent, and as such they continue to deserve a fair hearing among the international community of New Testament scholars. With that consideration in mind, the primary objective of this translation has been clarity. The overarching goal has been to make Schmidt's arguments accessible to those who may not have read them before.

That puzzling sentence from the beginning of Part Two can serve as a useful illustration. It comes amid Schmidt's discussion of the similarities and differences between the gospel passion narratives and early Christian martyr-acts. He is arguing that despite their apparent similarities, these two kinds of literature are essentially quite different: the gospel passion narratives were the product of "a living popular cultic tradition," but the martyr-acts were shaped by secular literary conventions, including well-known trial stories of Greek philosophers and Roman heroes. The telling of these "trial transcript" stories, Schmidt asserts, increasingly developed into an art form, or dramatic construction, in its own right. In this context he wrote:

> Dieser erhielt, je mehr neben den Märtyrer der Mönch, der Heilige in der kirchlichen Wertschätzung trat, den Sinn des Heiligenlebens, dessen innere Vorgänge hier in äussere umgesetzt sind.

Feel free to take a moment or two with that sentence. A very literal translation would run along these lines: "This received, the nearer to the martyr the monk, the saint in the church's esteem, stepped, the sense of the life of the saint, whose inner processes are here converted into externals." The translator of this sentence is confronted by two challenges: first, to determine what Schmidt most likely meant; and second, to express that meaning in reasonably clear English. Close attention to grammatical and syntactical connections shows that the basic structure of the sentence can be rendered: "As the monk, who was a saint in the estimation of the church, stepped nearer and nearer to the martyr, this [dramatic construction of the martyr's trial] received the sense of the life of a saint, whose inner processes were here brought into the open." Schmidt's point appears to be that as the growing monastic movement steadily raised the status of monks in the eyes of the church, the form of martyr-acts became increasingly stylized, until eventually they came to include a long speech by the martyr recounting his or her inner experiences. The monk and the martyr, in other words, came to look more and more alike. This statement, which might be open for discussion among historians of early Christian monasticism, serves as the capstone and conclusion to Schmidt's argument that the martyr-acts do not arise from the same kind of literary influences that produced the passion narratives of the gospels.

Since the goal of this translation has been to make Schmidt's arguments as clear as possible, the English version of this sentence should help the reader comprehend the point Schmidt wants to make without necessarily reproducing the overwrought complexity of his sentence structure. To that end, the English version printed here goes as follows:

> Indeed, as monks—whom the church regarded as saints—approached the status of martyrs, this dramatic construction came to have the sense of a life of the saint, bringing his or her inner experiences out into the open.

An English-speaking reader of that sentence might well want to take issue with the point that Schmidt is trying to make; perhaps here (as elsewhere, on occasion) Schmidt has painted with too broad a brush. Be that as it may, the translation will enable the reader to get an accurate understanding of the content of Schmidt's argument. And that has been the goal of this translation throughout— to clear away the obscurities of Schmidt's mode of expression without detracting from the power of his ideas.

In addition to highly complicated sentence structure, Schmidt also makes frequent use of technical terms, some of which are essential to his argument in *Die Stellung.* Three terms that recur throughout the book are basic to his outlook on the genre of the gospels, and because they pose various problems for translation, they need to be discussed briefly here: the nouns *Hochliteratur* and *Kleinliteratur,* and the adjective *volkstümlich.* The neologisms *Hochliteratur* and *Kleinliteratur* were coined by Schmidt to describe the two distinct categories that he regarded as essential to a correct literary appraisal of the gospels. *Hochliteratur,* on the one hand, was Schmidt's designation for documents that are the product of the creative efforts of an individual writer. Such documents are the work of a *Schriftstellerpersönlichkeit* (authorial personality) whose talents give shape and form to the written product. *Hochliteratur* is the artistic output of a human individual; it is, Schmidt declares, "actual literature" *(die eigentliche Literatur).* But *Kleinliteratur* is something quite different—not the work of an individual but the product of a collective, not the result of one person's labor but the outgrowth of a community's common life. *Kleinliteratur,* Schmidt asserts, is created by no one and by everyone; it comes from nowhere and from everywhere. It is "not a belabored product but a lush growth." Schmidt goes to great lengths to make the case that *Kleinliteratur,* as the written detritus of an oral tradition, has an autonomy that is immune to the creative interventions of any individual author. The Gospels are therefore not analogous to any other biographical literature from late antiquity.

This is not the place for a full discussion of Schmidt's distinction between *Hochliteratur* and *Kleinliteratur,* but it is important to explain how these technical terms have been handled in this translation. Many scholars who discuss *Die Stellung* choose not to translate these German terms. They are, after all, neologisms created by Schmidt to designate specialized literary categories. They are technical terms as well, and leaving them untranslated has the advantage of preserving that impression. This choice, however, fails to express the terms in English, and since the purpose of a translation is to move text from one language into another, keeping to Schmidt's German terminology amounts to a kind of admission of defeat on the part of the translator.

When the terms are translated in scholarly discussions, they are most often rendered as "high literature" and "low literature" respectively. These expressions have the advantage of sticking quite close to the original German and also of preserving in English the residual impression of a *terminus technicus.* They have the disadvantage, though, of introducing a possible connotation that was not present in Schmidt's argument. Specifically, the adjectives *high* and *low* can cause English-speaking readers to infer that these terms denote literature of superior and inferior quality. "High literature" sounds like a reference to classic literature, perhaps the "great" literature of human civilization; whereas "low literature" sounds like a reference to writings that are of less literary merit. Schmidt, of course, had nothing of the sort in mind.

He did, unfortunately, choose words that can carry that connotation even in German. The German word *hoch,* for example, means "high," and as such it can describe the elevation of everything from a person's age to an apartment's rent. In some contexts, *hoch* even carries the connotation of "noble" or "sublime," as in the expression *die hohe Woche* for Holy Week. Likewise, the German word *klein* literally means "small," and as such it can be used with reference to the modest size not only of people but also of places, towns, or villages. In some contexts it takes on the implication of "insignificant," as in the adjective *kleinlich,* "petty, paltry." The fact that the translations "high literature" and "low literature" can elicit impressions of superiority and inferiority, then, is not an argument against the appropriateness of their use as translations of *Hochliteratur* and *Kleinliteratur.* On the contrary, it argues in their favor. For the expressions "high literature" and "low literature" are likely to draw from an English-speaking reader a response very close to that evoked in German by Schmidt's original terminology. Accordingly, "high literature" and "low literature" are used throughout this translation wherever *Hochliteratur* and *Kleinliteratur* appear in the German text.

The adjective *volkstümlich* poses a different kind of difficulty. Here the English translation closest at hand ("popular") carries a connotation that is, in fact, quite different from what Schmidt wrote. Schmidt uses *volkstümlich* to describe a quality that he believed inhered in the gospels because of their origins in a community setting. To Schmidt, the gospels are "popular" because they arise from the common life of a group. The gospels, he argues, are a sociological phenomenon, the effluence of an oral tradition. In using the term *volkstümlich,* then, he is claiming that the creative energy that produced the gospels came, not from their authors, but from the life of a religious community. Behind the gospels lies, not the intelligence and effort of a *Schriftstellerpersönlichkeit,* but the dynamic (and, Schmidt thought, cultic) experience of a *Volk.* In English, however, the word *popular* does not mean, in spite of its etymology, "arising from the people." English speakers today use this word to refer to things which are common to, or known and enjoyed by, large numbers of people. To call the gospels "popular" in that sense would appear to declare that they had a wide circulation. Schmidt, of course, would never have made that assertion about the gospels. Accordingly, this translation often uses other words where *volkstümlich* appears in the German text, preferring instead English expressions that evoke the impression of a community, including "communal," "collective," and "folk."

Acknowledgments

I am grateful to a number of people without whose help and kindness this project never would have found its way to completion. Erika Scavillo, as I mention in my introduction, helped at several key points, and if it had not been for my friend Jonathan Reed of the University of LaVerne, I might still be wondering what the German expression "to paint ghosts on the wall" really means. D. Moody Smith of Duke University first saw the value of this project and provided wise guidance all along the way, while the graduate students in the New Testament seminar at Duke University read an earlier version of the translation and offered constructive criticisms. Anonymous readers also sharpened the translation, and Barry Blose of the University of South Carolina Press has been a patient and merciful editor from the very beginning. Most of all I am grateful to my wife, Linda, who listened with apparent interest whenever I talked about K. L. Schmidt. With so many capable helpers, this translation should not contain any errors at all, so those which persist must be laid squarely on my doorstep. It is my sincere hope that they are not serious enough to prevent interested readers from engaging with the important ideas in this monograph.

BYRON R. MCCANE

PART ONE

Description and critique of previous attempts to determine the place of the gospels in the general history of literature

GREEK BIOGRAPHICAL LITERATURE: LIVES OF PHILOSOPHERS, DIOGENES LAERTIUS, CONTEMPORANEOUS HISTORIOGRAPHY, XENOPHON'S *MEMORABILIA* (JESUS AND SOCRATES, JUSTIN AND THE GOSPELS, PAPIAS AND THE GOSPELS, JUSTIN AND PAPIAS), PERIPATETIC AND ALEXANDRIAN BIOGRAPHY.

There is no shortage of attempts to examine the gospels from the standpoint of the general history of world literature. In what follows, I will cite and criticize the important opinions—or at least those that are regarded as important.

Understandably, comparison of the gospels with the roughly contemporaneous Greek biographical literature has enjoyed particular popularity, with the American Clyde Weber Votaw offering the most detailed treatment.[1] His very broad presentation, which is (as I expected) unencumbered by interaction with the scholarly literature, starts in the right place and offers a number of good observations. In the end, however, it does not deliver what it promises. It is much too general and even contains some things that are misleading.

Obviously, as "brief, special, and popular writings," the gospels stand out starkly from the contemporary high literature generally known to us. As "writings of the people, by the people, and for the people," they belong neither to historical nor to philosophical literature. Since the gospels do represent biography of some sort, however, we need to clarify the essence of ancient biography. In Weber Votaw's opinion, there were two types: precise, objective, historical biography; and practical, pedagogical, popular biography. The latter type, which was largely confined to antiquity (as opposed to more recent periods), depicts and glorifies specific heroes. Popular biographies of this sort were especially plentiful during the centuries immediately before and after Christ, including (among others) Xenophon's *Memorabilia,* Arrian's *Epictetus,* and Philostratus's *Apollonius of Tyana.* These three documents are the closest parallels to the gospels, so the argument goes. The inadequacy of Weber Votaw's method is plain to see: the difference between the two types of biography has not been

---

1. C. W. Votaw, "The Gospels and Contemporary Biographies," *American Journal of Theology* 19 (1915): 45–73, 217–49.

clearly thought out. What Xenophon, Arrian, and Philostratus have in common must be marked off more sharply. As a group, they are different from the evangelists because they reveal specific authorial personalities. Despite a good start, then, what Weber Votaw has produced is simply not a literary-historical evaluation of the gospels. Instead, the whole project boils down to the same old comparison of Jesus with Socrates, Epictetus, and Apollonius.

Similar mistakes—such as, looking at content instead of the literary background—also occur in the work of C. F. G. Heinrici.[2] He stresses that "the value, content, and individuality of the traditions is most clearly recognizable through comparison with related works," but then he wanders off the path of literary-historical comparison by asserting that "the best such comparisons are found not in fables like Callisthenes' Alexander novel or the apocryphal Acts of early Christianity, but in serious biographies of people who were filled with the desire to strive or to intercede for the eternal good of the world." Heinrici thinks that these biographies—principally those of philosophers—deal with people who wanted to proclaim to their followers (indeed, to all humankind) a philosophy of life that would produce bliss and contentment. This aim touches on that of the gospels: in an important sense, both are books with a religious orientation. Be that as it may, it sheds very little light on the formation and essence of the gospels. For Heinrici whittles the whole comparative method down to the question of content—the relation between the εὐαγγέλλιον and the δόξαι τῶν φιλοσόφων, the message of Jesus and the teaching of the philosophers, the story of Jesus and the stories of the philosophers. So earnestly does he want to bring the two together that he overlooks the obvious differences between them; and as a result, the comparison ends up running aground. It can hardly be otherwise, though, when attention to form is disregarded in favor of content, because the form of the gospels is quite different from the form of the ancient philosophical biographies. Thus, the same criticisms that were made of Weber Votaw must also be leveled against Heinrici.

Well, perhaps not entirely. Heinrici does draw attention to a significant point of formal comparison.[3] He finds that the gospels are reminiscent of Xenophon's *Memorabilia* and the biographies of philosophers by Diogenes Laertius (and others) because in both cases there is a collection of material. This observation—hardly original to Heinrici—is both correct and important. The distinguishing characteristic here is that disconnected *apophthegmata* have been networked together, with various sorts of anecdotes filling in the gaps. The result is that many ancient philosophers' lives are highly perforated in their structure, appearing to be nothing but a compilation of different traditions, a "patchwork of significant words and deeds of the hero" (as Heinrici rightly puts it). This fact is undeniable and does remind us of the gospels.

2. C. F. G. Heinrici, "Die Bodenständigkeit der synoptischen Überlieferung," *Biblische Zeit und Streitfragen* 8.11 (1913): 5ff.

3. C. F. G. Heinrici, *Der literarische Charakter der neutestamentlichen Schriften* (1908), 36.

But at this point we must be careful not to jump to the wrong conclusion: judged from a scientific point of view, Diogenes Laertius was an incompetent biographer,[4] for he haphazardly produced a great number biographies (they were more like rapidly dictated, uneven leaflets!), whereas the gospel tradition was a natural process—not a belabored product but a lush growth. The same standard of judgment cannot possibly be applied to both the gospels and Diogenes Laertius, since he tries to pass himself off as an author, writing a long foreword and naming his sources, and still manages to produce an incoherent work. There is no comparison between Diogenes Laertius and any of the gospels, not even Luke.

A different question, to which we will return, is whether or not such biographies weave together individual pieces and small collections that would correspond to the gospels in their preliminary stages. Despite their critical awareness, then, the Alexandrian biographies did not sift through the disharmony of the popular traditions but only collected them.[5] But since they sought to be scholarly (and they were, if their diligence and the wealth of their material is taken into account), they must be judged differently from the evangelists.

Something else is lacking from the gospels that cannot be explained through ancient biographical literature, or for that matter, through any connection with that literature. We know that in the gospels there are internal chronological gaps and evident psychological lapses; moreover, we find not the slightest trace of development in the hero. Hero development is also generally lacking from ancient biographies.[6] This fact has led one recent commentator on the Gospel of Luke[7] to think that the third gospel (which he takes to be a "life-story in the contemporary historiographers' sense of the term"[8]) belongs in the category of ancient historiography, with its undeveloped characters and legendary embellishments. But it is not at all clear why this feature of Luke, which he shares with Mark and Matthew, has to be explained with reference to a genre of ancient literature. That kind of thinking stands and falls with the mistaken opinion that Luke was an ancient historiographer like Polybius or Eusebius.

4. Cf. the analysis offered by Eduard Schwartz in Pauly-Wissowa-Kroll, *Realenzyklopädie der klassischen Altertumswissenschaft* (s.v. Diogenes Laertius). It appears to me that in his analysis of the Gospel of John ("Aporias in the Fourth Gospel," *Nachrichten von der Gesellschaft der Wissenschaften zu Göttingen*, 1908), he feels the full force of the method that he correctly employed in relation to Diogenes Laertius. He cannot express enough surprise at the contradictions within the Gospel of John; he can only judge them to be "nonsensical, atrocious, outrageous, insipid." He does not have the ability to "untangle this chaos," this "Babylonian mess."

5. A. Gercke and E. Norden, *Einleitung in die Altertumswissenschaft* (1912), 266f.

6. "The ancient biographers hardly ever even thought of it" (v. Wilamowitz-Möllendorf, *Die Kultur der Gegenwart* [1907]), 118.

7. V. O. Janssen, *Der literarische Charakter des Lukasevangeliums* (doctoral diss., Jena [1917]), 7ff.

8. For Eduard Meyer (*Ursprung und Anfänge des Christentums*, 1921), this slightly perverse judgment of Luke is straightforward and obvious. He thinks that because they

It is Johannes Weiss who has brought the real literary question into sharper focus.[9] Drawing on the pertinent work of Hirzel[10] and Ivo Bruns,[11] Weiss has given a preliminary description of the genre of ancient memoirs, the parade example of which is Xenophon's *Memorabilia* (ἀπομνημονεύματα, "memoirs"— not ὑπομνήματα, "memories"). This literary genre typically moves back and forth between narration and dialogue, so that the order of the material lacks both internal and external connections. Anecdotes, episodes, dialogues, and individual sayings are all loosely linked up into a narrative framework. It is particularly significant that the connections between episodes may not necessarily be made clear. Often, for example, the setting for a scene about a conversation of Socrates is introduced by only a brief protasis or participial construction. This pattern is similar to Matthew, who loves to set the background of a scene with a brief participial construction and then put a saying or story of Jesus strongly in the foreground. Mark and Luke (especially) have a different style.[12] But like them, Xenophon does not always make the connection with previous events explicit. So there are parallels here between the memoirs and the gospels.

All of this is exactly the opposite of what we would expect from practical biography, and in this regard the gospels and the memoirs are in full accord. On the other hand, a crucial characteristic of memoirs is the way the author seems to want to step forward as a personality, authenticating the material, listing sources, naming informants, and developing the plot. This feature is completely lacking in Mark and is largely absent from all the other gospels as well. Of course, in later gospels the literary "I" steps forward with increasing prominence, so that those documents come somewhat closer to memoir literature. But Johannes Weiss rightly sees that earlier gospels are different.

Others who have addressed this question have agreed. Wendland[13] argues that the value of both Xenophon's *Memorabilia* and Arrian's *Epictetus* depends

---

stand out from the original traditions as fixed compositions, the speeches in Matthew are "analogous to the great speeches which Greek and Roman historians since Thucydides have put into the mouths of the personalities they deal with." I have to regard this opinion as completely wrong. Notwithstanding their more or less artful composition, the Matthean speeches belong in the realm of early Christian parenesis. In that realm the community was more important than the author's personality.

9. Johannes Weiss, *Das älteste Evangelium* (1903), 5ff., 150. Cf. also Weiss's *Jesus von Nazareth, Mythus oder Geschichte?* (1910), 127f.

10. Hirzel, *Der Dialog* (1895), I.144. [Schmidt's citation is incomplete here, probably because Weiss's footnote in *Das älteste Evangelium* was incomplete as well. Schmidt exactly reproduces Weiss's citation, nothing more. Trans.].

11. Ivo Bruns, *Das literarische Porträt der Griechen im 5. und 4. Jahrhundert* (1896), 372.

12. Cf. the collected examples in my book, *Der Rahmen der Geschichte Jesu*, esp. the table on p. 319, "Participial Constructions in the Introductions to the Pericopes of Matthew."

13. P. Wendland, *Die urchristlichen Literaturformen* (1912), 266.

entirely upon the personality of the author. Bauernfeind[14] sees the *Memorabilia* as only a species of the biographical literature, about which more will be said later. Dibelius[15] quotes Wendland. Hans von Soden asserts: "The Gospels are, in our judgment, of an anecdotal character. They do not have—and were never intended to have—any formal kinship with either ancient biographies or ancient memoirs."[16] Bultmann[17] points out that a gospel, unlike a memoir or a Hellenistic biography, lacks both a real biographical interest and the technique to carry it out.[18] A very recent commentator on the literary form of the Gospels, C. Bouma of Holland,[19] agrees with Weiss and rightly draws attention to the fact that in contrast to the *Memorabilia,* the gospels unceremoniously put sayings and actions side by side in the foreground. Moreover, in Xenophon's work most of the people who speak with Socrates are named, whereas in the gospels most of those who speak with Jesus are anonymous: Jesus takes up all of the spotlight and stands more at center stage than Socrates.

It has already been noted that comparisons of the gospels and Xenophon's *Memorabilia* are basically nothing more than comparisons of Jesus with Socrates. This fact makes one wonder whether literary criticism of the gospels has not been too greatly influenced by questions of content. "Jesus Christ and Socrates: these two names represent the dearest memories of the human race"—Adolf von Harnack's[20] words aptly illustrate why the stories of these two personalities always seem to stand alongside each other.[21] Neither one of them ever wrote anything; instead, they exercised their influence through teaching, living, and dying. For the entire first century, we hear nothing at all in Christian circles about Socrates. He is mentioned for the first time around the middle of the second century, and from then on he regularly appears, usually in references that

14. O. Bauernfeind, *Die literarische Form des Evangeliums,* Ph.D. diss., Greifswald (1915), 7.

15. Martin Dibelius, *From Tradition to Gospel,* trans. B. L. Woolf (Cambridge, Clarke, 1971), 40.

16. H. von Soden, "Die Entstehung der christlichen Kirche," *Aus Natur und Geisteswelt* 690 (1919): 72.

17. Rudolf Bultmann, *Die Geschichte der synoptischen Tradition* (1921), 228. [Schmidt refers here to the 1921 German edition of Bultmann's classic work; the standard English translation by John Marsh, however, is based on the fifth edition and does not include this particular quotation. Trans.]

18. In this regard, Bultmann also mentions "a collection of anecdotes like the life of Aesop" and seems to want to find there the biographical techniques that he does not find in the gospels. On this matter, and on the connection Bultmann draws between the gospels, myth, and cult, more is to be said later.

19. C. Bouma, *De literarische vorm der Evangelien,* Ph.D. diss., Amsterdam (1921), 149ff.

20. Adolf von Harnack, *Sokrates und die alte Kirche* (1900); later reprinted in *Reden und Aufsätze* (1906).

21. For more Harnackesque comments, cf. esp. F. C. Baur, *Sokrates und Christus* (1876).

adduce Xenophon's *Memorabilia* as a parallel to the gospels. Justin, ever the apologist for Christianity, links Jesus closely with Socrates and refers to the gospels more than a dozen times as ἀπομνημονεύματα τῶν ἀποστόλων,[22] the very word Xenophon had chosen for the title of his book about Socrates. That Justin actually had Xenophon's work in mind cannot be conclusively proved from any of his writings, but in an addendum to his *Second Apology* (10–11) he contrasts Jesus with Socrates and then immediately quotes a lengthy citation from Xenophon's *Memorabilia*. So there can be little doubt that he meant to call to mind this archetype of the memoir genre.

Justin's opinion not only affected other early Christian authors but has even influenced modern scholars of the gospels, a fact most clearly illustrated by Theodor Zahn, who first describes the early Christian ideas of the comparison between Jesus and Socrates and then goes on to make the comparison himself with great vigor. Zahn and his followers feel confident about this conception of the gospels, even though I myself have completely rejected it any number of times. In Justin the apologetic outlook is decisive: he is determined to elevate the cultural level of Christianity, and to that end he employs the designation "memoirs" to locate the gospels in the high literature. Zahn virtually says as much when he asserts, "The name was excellently chosen and aptly suited to give literary-minded Gentiles the right picture of the genre of the Gospels."[23] But there is something else that matters even more to Zahn: for him the term *apomnemoneumata* is the surest confirmation of the reliability of the Gospels, since it means that they must have actually been "memoirs" of the apostles, just like Xenophon's "memoirs" of Socrates.

> The comparison was as apt as it was understandable. Gospels can be considered to have been written by the disciples of Jesus if they are based on the disciples' running notes of what they experienced with Jesus and heard from him. In the gospels there are stories which were not directly experienced by the Evangelist in question, but by other disciples, and there are also things which actually derive not from the Evangelists' own memories (since the Evangelists were only students of the apostles), but rather from what had survived in the memory of their teachers, the original witnesses. Thus the name "memoirs of the apostles" was perfectly justified. Even Xenophon's classic work contained material which came not from his own memory but from unknown sources.[24]

It lies beyond Zahn's field of vision to notice that the gospel tradition was formed in the primitive Christian community and that, since the evangelists

---

22. A thorough discussion of these references appears in Theodor Zahn, *Geschichte des neutestamentlichen Kanons* (1889), 466f. The citations themselves are printed in E. Preuschen, *Antilegomena* (1905), 33ff.

23. Zahn, *Geschichte des neutestamentlichen Kanons*, 471.

24. Ibid., 473f.

compiled it, we have to distinguish between tradition and composition. As far as Zahn is concerned, the evangelists were not collectors but essentially direct witnesses. He does not explicitly say that the gospels are representative of ancient high literature, but it is important to Zahn that they have the same sure authority in relation to Jesus that Xenophon has in relation to Socrates.

Zahn understandably places great value on the fact that even though Justin was the first to refer to Xenophon's *Memorabilia,* he was not the first to think of the gospels as ἀπομνημονεύματα. In his judgment, the apostles had predecessors as (ἀπο)μνημονεύοντες. Justin "traded a technical ecclesiastical term for a label which would have been understandable to a non-Christian reader, but in no way did he deviate from the church's view of the gospels: he only added a term which had already spread rather widely within the church."[25] In this regard, the famous statement of Papias, particularly his comment about Mark, becomes extremely significant: Μάρκος . . . ἑρμηνευτὴς Πέτρον γενόμενος, ὅσα ἐμνημόνευσεν, ἀκριβῶς ἔγραψεν . . . οὕτως ἔνια γράψας ὡς ἀπεμνημόνευσεν (Eusebius, *EH* III.39). Here the verb (ἀπο)μνημονεύειν clearly means the written record of a recollection.

Zahn is not the only one who sets great store by the reliability of such individual recollections. Recently Eduard Meyer has reached the same conclusion in his book that I have already mentioned. His method of examining the gospels is insufficient precisely because it is simply the result of his loyalty to Papias.[26] And how did Papias go wrong? In the same way that Justin did: by placing the gospels in the category of actual literature. He made Mark out to be the first messenger and writer of the Jesus story, even though the literary shape of Mark's gospel rules out any chance that it could possibly have originated with one individual. Since Meyer cannot deny that the Gospel of Mark lacks all traces of personal color, he tries to solve this riddle by psychoanalyzing Peter and supposing that Peter was so humble that he only told stories of true events. In actual fact, the spreading tradition, anonymous as it was, had absolutely no interest in personal details. Only in the wake of Papias did there arise an interest in adding personal memories to a tradition that had previously been entirely free of such influences. Finally, there is also the fact that chronology and psychology are completely lacking in Mark's gospel: they have to be read into it. If you want to follow Papias, that is what you must do.

It is significant that Papias and Justin differ in the degree of confidence with which they speak of "memoirs" of the apostles. While Justin is certain that the gospels do belong to this literary genre, Papias takes only a few steps in that direction. From his somewhat tortuous description of the origin of Mark's gospel, it appears that in Papias's mind the ideal gospel would be a document in

25. Ibid., 474f.

26. Cf., among others, my criticism of Meyer's book in *Die christliche Welt* (1921), 114ff. M. Dibelius makes even sharper remarks on this topic in *Deutsche Literaturzeitung* (1921), 225ff. He regards Meyer's evaluation of the quotation as a relapse into outdated methods.

which an eyewitness had recorded his memories. But that is not what Mark is. The author of Mark was only an indirect witness to the story of Jesus, and his gospel cannot properly be called a "memoir." Papias recognizes that Mark lacks chronological order from the very start, but he explains this "deficit" as the result of Peter's practical didactic purpose: sometimes he told one story, and sometimes he told another. Justin put these positive insights into total eclipse. He was in the unenviable position of having to make the gospel (peculiar as it was) understandable as literature not only to non-Christian bystanders but also to himself, because in an important sense the gospels—the "so-called" gospels (ἃ καλεῖται εὐαγγέλλια; τὸ λεγόμενον εὐαγγέλλιον)—were strange to Justin too. In so doing, he blocked the way (both for himself and for those who followed him) to a proper literary understanding of the gospels, because he took them out of the context of the primitive Christian community in which their literary form was shaped. Papias at least had some knowledge of the practical didactic purposes that influenced the arrangement of the Jesus story, but he still began the process of "literature-izing" the gospels. By designating the gospels as ἀπομνημονεύματα of particular individual personalities, both Papias and Justin (but especially Justin) "put things in the wrong social sphere: the second and third generations introduced material that had more of the feel of secular literary activity. They may have been hoping for the end of the world, but they were actually working for the sake of posterity."[27]

That is the only conclusion that can possibly be reached, however, if the gospels are linked with Xenophon's *Memorabilia* (a book that is, by the way, not only the archetype of the memoir genre but also its sole surviving exemplar). Low literature is simply not the same as high literature. The situation might be different if there were some scholarly doubt about whether ἀπομνημονεύματα really belonged to high literature. R. Reitzenstein[28] offered the following definition during his discussion of the documents related to *Apollonius of Tyana*. Pointing to the ἀπομνημονεύματα of Moiragenes—"a book corresponding to Acts," he says —Reitzenstein comments: "The title is used in philosophical and magical texts (cf. the recitation of magic divine names in Dieterich *Abraxas* 202: ἐν δὲ τοῖς Εὐήνου ἀπομνημονεύμασιν ὁ λέγει (λέγεις Pap.) παρὰ τοῖς Αἰγυπτίοις Σύροις φωνεῖσθαι· χθεθωνί) We should expect sayings or miracle stories or even, as in the Pythagoras aretalogy, both. For Justin, the gospels are ἀπομνημονεύματα too."[29] Reitzenstein adds: "If we had the Moiragenes document, we would probably be swamped by constant comparisons with the gospels, especially the Fourth."[30] His conclusion is right, but not his reference to Justin. As I have already explained, Justin did not think of the gospels as religious low literature, but rather as the great literary work of someone like Xenophon.

27. Dibelius, *Deutsche Literaturzeitung*, 232.
28. R. Reitzenstein, *Hellenistische Wundererzählungen* (1906), 40.
29. Ibid., 53.
30. This has been correctly elaborated by Zahn, *Geschichte des neutestamentlichen Kanons*, 473.

To this point our discussion has shown that the gospels belong neither to high literature nor to biographical literature more broadly speaking. In addition, the inadequacies of previous investigations into this subject have been exposed. There is, however, a work by Johannes Weiss[31] that must be mentioned here, because it draws attention to an important point of comparison between the gospels and one branch of ancient biographical literature: peripatetic biographies. Weiss recognizes that at substantial and decisive points the Gospel of Mark stops short of biography. Biographies have an interest in the upbringing and family background of the hero, and they also describe the hero's physical appearance and character. All of this is missing from Mark. Only in later evangelists does a turn toward biography first begin to appear, and it seems to me that Weiss makes too much of these beginnings. Even if the gospels of Matthew and Luke do have birth narratives, that does not mean they stand any closer to biography than Mark does, for they do not have the conscious biographical method that one finds in genuine biographies. But Weiss sees an analogy between Mark and the peripatetic biographies, particularly in the way in which Mark characterizes Jesus.

Along with F. Leo,[32] Weiss distinguishes between peripatetic biographies (Plutarch is the classic example) and the Alexandrian grammarian lives, which Suetonius picked up and converted from literary to political purposes for the caesars. While those documents offer a description of the hero's personality according to a set schema, the peripatetic biographies characterize the hero merely by illustrating his ἦθος through his πράξεις In Mark a description or sketch of Jesus is almost completely absent: it is his πράξεις which are emphasized. "Readers can draw their own conclusions," Weiss asserts. "There can be no doubt that our work belongs to the peripatetic line of development (hence it is also certainly akin to Xenophon's *Memorabilia*)."[33] Later he expands on Jesus' prominence in the Gospel of Mark and concludes: "The Evangelist employed some small devices to make it all stand out more clearly. The most notable of these is a device frequently used in ancient literature, i.e., indirect characterization."[34] With regard to the account of the first miracle of Jesus in Capernaum he writes: "Here in the opening debut of the Son of God we find the first example of indirect characterization, which Mark loves and which ancient authors had developed into a special art form."[35]

There can be no doubt that Weiss has identified an important property of the Gospel of Mark—and of gospels in general—but he has evaluated it all wrong. One should not ask whether Mark stands in the line of peripatetic biography; such a question bears absolutely no fruit for understanding the gospels. On that

31. J. Weiss, *Das älteste Evangelium* (1903), 11ff.
32. F. Leo, *Die griechische-römische Biographie* (1901).
33. Weiss, *Das älteste Evangelium*, 12.
34. Ibid., 16.
35. Ibid., 150.

view, any book of legends, any folk book, or practically any other example of low literature that describes the hero only through his words and deeds would have to be related to the peripatetic method. But the peripatetics were self-conscious and artificial, whereas the gospels, legends, and folk books developed through an unconscious process, which grew up all on its own.[36]

It is significant that Johannes Weiss stops short of drawing any direct connection between the gospels and the development of the peripatetic biographies. To him there is one supremely important detail by which the gospels stand out strongly from ancient biographies: "The physical appearance of the redeemer was so utterly insignificant that the tradition recorded nothing about it. That is a sign that the tradition could not have arisen under Greek influences, since on this point they were not indifferent."[37] Both parts of that sentence are only half true at

---

36. It is quite a different matter that some ancient Christian lives of the saints were indeed written by philosophically educated men of letters and thus do work with elements of the peripatetic method. Cf. H. Mertel, *Die biographische Form der greichischen Heiligenlegenden*, Ph.D. diss., Munich (1909). According to Mertel, Athanasius's *Life of Antony* was constructed along the lines of Plutarch's peripatetic biographies. Even though his interest in pious edification usually causes Athanasius to fall short of the compact peripatetic style, his work still exemplifies the typical form of a Plutarchian *bios*. Of course it is true that the various *bioi* that followed Athanasius were in the genre of artistic prose. An exception is Leontius's popular seventh-century legend of John, which is not artistic hagiography but rather highly novelistic and anecdotal. It is "not a life but only an outline of a life of the saint, consistently fulfilling the purpose of which a folk writer must always be cognizant, i.e., to narrate clearly and simply" (Mertel, 90). After Mertel's assessment of the *Life of Antony* met with widespread approval, K. Holl raised important objections to it in an article entitled "Die schriftstellerische Form des griechischen Heiligenlebens" in *Neue Jahrbücher für das klassische Altertum* (1912), 406ff. Holl identified a consistent internal form in the *Life of Antony* and asserted that "one has to look far and wide in antiquity to find a document which can be compared with it for rigor of style and artistic consistency." R. Reitzenstein, on the other hand, lodged a protest against Holl's conclusions in his paper "Des Athanasius Werk über das Leben des Antonius: Ein Beitrag zur Geschichte des Mönchtums," which was published in *Sitzungsberichte der Heidelberger Akademie der Wissenschaften* (1914). He did not see Holl's inner development in the *Life of Antony*, but rather something more superficial, merely a development in geography: "There is no development in the plot. That stagnates—indeed, it has to. But miracle stories and visions are richly interwoven with a certain superficial knack (until chap. 66). This is a typical monk story, as we know them so well from the *Historia Lausiaca* and Rufinus's *Historia Monachorum*, or Jerome's *Life of Hilary*" (20). Thus Reitzenstein brings Athanasius's work closer to religious low literature and certainly does not hold to the view that Athanasius knew the genre of the ancient *bios*. It seems to me that Reitzenstein has gotten it essentially right. His opposition to Holl has programmatic significance for gospel researchers, who have to work in this field with all these disputed questions at the same time: artistic literature vs. low literature, composition vs. tradition, and the transmission of a literary plot through an authorial personality.

37. Weiss, *Das älteste Evangelium*, 15.

best. Nothing is said of Jesus' external appearance simply because the tradition is thoroughly esoteric. Low literature cannot be played off against high literature. What Weiss found only in Judaism is also there in Hellenism, as long as one looks at folk books and such.

2

JUDAISM AND HELLENISM, ARAMAIC FOLK BOOKS, ANCIENT AND MODERN ORIENTALIA, RABBINICS, THE HEBREW BIBLE.

Quite apart from these technical questions, is it not obvious that analogies to the gospels should be sought in Jewish sources? Should we not begin by assuming that, despite their Greek dress, the gospels are Jewish products? As a matter of fact, Judaism does offer some noteworthy comparisons. H. Gressmann has drawn attention to Aramaic folk books of the pre-Christian era, all of which were lost until the Ahikar novel was discovered among the Elephantine papyri: "This example by itself is sufficient proof that folk books like Aramaic gospels did circulate in the pre-Christian era, and that they had the same literary character as the Ahikar novel (i.e., the distinctive combination of wisdom sayings—maxims, fables, parables—with a narrative). It does not really matter whether they were pure adventure novels (Ahikar) or semi-historical biographies laced with miracle stories (Gospel)."[38]

Gressmann's literary-historical judgment, which we will take up further below, works with a clear and correct idea: folk books bring together words *and* deeds. In addition, it must also be noted that the tradition of the Ahikar fable is extremely complicated. Widely known because it is found in some recensions of *The 1001 Nights,* the story exists not only in Arabic but also in Syriac, Armenian, and Slavic versions. Its presence among the Aramaic Elephantine papyri[39] confirms that it is very old. The title of the Elephantine text, "Maxims of a Wise and Intelligent Writer by the Name of Ahikar, Which He Taught to His Son," shows that the major emphasis fell on the sayings and that the narrative simply provided a framework.[40] But perhaps the title also shows that the Ahikar story (which, even though it is the oldest tale we have from Semitic soil, can surely be traced back even further) was handed down only in excerpts. The content of the narrative was constantly changing as it was handed down in the tradition.

38. H. Gressmann, "Vom reichen Mann und armen Lazarus," *Abhandlungen der Berliner Akademie der Wissenschaften* (1918): 3ff.

39. E. Sachau, *Aramäische Papyrus und Ostraka aus einer jüdischen Militärkolonie zu Elephantine* (1911); A. Ungnad, *Aramäische Papyrus aus Elephantine* (1911).

40. Fr. Stummer disagrees in his *Der kritische Wert der altaramäischen Ahikar-Texte aus Elephantine* (1914). He argues that the sayings collection was arranged later,

For gospel researchers it is especially important that from an early date the various recensions had the maxims in different orders; it is the maxims, then, that are the true core and basis of the entire work. It can be very instructive to compare the order of the maxims in the four main recensions named above.[41] In addition to variations in the length of the maxims (here the tendency to shorten is every bit as apparent as the tendency to lengthen; cf. the contents of the gospel logia), there are also differences in the order of the maxims when they appear in two or more recensions (here the analogy with the various gospels applies again). On the whole, the Ahikar tradition[42] seems sometimes more and sometimes less complicated than the gospel tradition. It seems more complicated when the course of the Ahikar tradition, which ran for many centuries, is compared with the relatively rapid development of a few gospels into a canon. But it seems less complicated when the relative simplicity of the Ahikar story is compared with the multiplicity of the gospel tradition.

At this point, Gressmann's recommendation that gospel folk books should be compared with the Ahikar folk book becomes problematic. Certainly it is right that in both cases there is a mixture of maxims and narrative, but the later versions of the Ahikar legend have a long series of maxims in only two places: at the beginning and at the end; first admonitions and then rebukes. It seems doubtful that this arrangement prevailed in the ancient Aramaic version;[43] probably the maxims were all consolidated in one place, supplemented by various fables. After all, the narrative does flow along quite logically and smoothly. This simple structure fits the single basic motive of the work, which is made plain at the end: if you dig a hole for your neighbor, you will fall into it yourself. Obviously

---

not only because in early versions the sayings do not always appear in the same place, but also because the sayings are mingled with fables, and most of all because the teachings of the sayings collection bear no relation to the situation of the narrator. He concludes that "the original Ahikar novel contained neither sayings nor fables, but either together or separately, each existed in close proximity to the other." I believe that a definite judgment cannot be made here. That is also the case with the sayings collection(s) in the gospels. What can be said with certainty about the existence of the Jesus sayings collection in an earlier period (i.e., sayings sources in Matthew and Luke: source or document?) or in a later period (Oxyrhynchus papyri)?

41. W. Bousset has offered just such a thorough comparison, including tables, in his "Beiträgen zur Ahikar-Legende," *ZNW* 16 (1905): 180ff.

42. A lucid presentation that assembles and organizes a great deal of Ahikar research is B. Meissner's *Das Märchen vom weisen Achiqar* (1917). Bousset's study, which I referred to a moment ago, is not mentioned by Meissner. In the same year as Meissner, Emil Grünberg's work appeared: *Die weisen Sprüche des Achikar nach der syrischen Hs. Cod. Sachau Nr. 336*, a dissertation at Giessen supervised by P. Kahle. Another disputed question that is brought to light by the complexity of the Ahikar tradition is its relationship to the Aesop story; cf. A. Hausrath, *Sitzungsberichten der Heidelberger Akademie der Wissenschaften* (1918).

43. A definitive answer to this question is not quite possible on the basis of the Sachau edition mentioned in the previous note.

the message and structure of the gospels is not so simple and cannot be so quickly circumscribed. Hence, the comparison between the gospels and the Ahikar story is only half correct, a limit that is not to be disregarded. The gospels are a collection of words and deeds. The emphasis of the Ahikar novel falls on the sayings. Despite its narrative framework, it belongs in the category of wisdom literature.[44]

In order to understand "Gospel folk books" it is important to observe carefully those parallels which illustrate a nonliterary tradition: short stories and light practical proverbs (which correspond to the individual pieces of the gospel tradition), and collections, frameworks, and explanations of such stories and proverbs (which correspond to the gospels as wholes). It is the second kind of parallel that interests us here. But the first—which gives the second its distinctive look—will also be considered. M. Dibelius recalls ancient and modern oriental parallels.[45] The oldest individual narratives of the gospel tradition betray no literary intention, no artistic outlook, no really personal perceptions, no external explanation, and no internal motivation. "Whoever wants to be persuaded that this kind of oral tradition still thrives in the Orient today, has only to read the stories collected by Hans Schmidt and Dschirius Jusif during the winter of 1910/11 among the peasants of Bir Zeit in the mountains of Ephraim . . . doubtless the best example of a popular tradition from recent times."[46] But right away Dibelius rightly sets a limit for the comparison: certainly both the gospel narratives and the Palestinian narratives are popular, but the gospels are borne along by a pronounced inclination toward propaganda (they want to make converts), whereas the Palestinian narratives simply want to entertain, nothing more. The gospel units have a devotional style and stand under a more earnest discipline than the Palestinian folk narratives, which come off with playful freedom.

Dibelius wonders whether the rabbinic tradition might be used as an analogy for this characteristic of the gospel reports, but immediately he notices an important difference here too: the creation and collection—or at the very least the sifting—of the rabbinic material was done by educated people, whereas the Christian tradition largely belonged to the uneducated. The legal tradition operated normatively among rabbis, whereas the earliest Christian narratives—the

44. Cf. Eduard Meyer, *Der Papyrusfund von Elephantine* (1912), 116: "The stories only provide settings or occasions for Ahikar to hold forth his wisdom. They are a narrative framework. Like so many other collections of oriental legends, this one also seeks first and foremost to give instruction, or (as in the case of Aesop's fables, which originally belonged to a 'life of Aesop') to give the settings in which he told the individual stories." In a footnote Meyer adds: "The Egyptian story of the maxims of the countryman belongs here as well, as does the Life of Homer with its mosaic of poems, maxims, and verse-riddles in emulation of Hesiod."

45. M. Dibelius, *From Tradition to Gospel*, 288.

46. Dibelius refers here to Hans Schmidt and P. Kahle, "Volkserzählungen aus Palästina," *Forschungen zur Religion und Literatur des Alten und Neuen Testaments* (1915, 1930), 17–18.

paradigms—were firmly rooted in preaching. It is different with the primitive Christian paranesis (sayings tradition), which developed directly out of Judaism. As a result, rabbinic anecdotes from the Talmudic tradition can, under certain strict conditions, serve as formal parallels to the gospel units. When A. Schlatter adduced the tradition of Johanan ben Zakkai as a parallel, he also added a limitation that rightly recognizes the difference in content even as it completely misses the difference in form: "The successors to ben Zakkai had nothing from him in writing: no long legal opinions or exegetical interpretations carried his name. There were only individual actions, מעשים, and aphorisms. Thus the form of the tradition about ben Zakkai is very closely related to the gospels. Stylistically, there is no closer parallel, as the recollections of the actions and words of a first-century teacher, than the casuistic literature. Spiritually, of course, they have almost nothing in common."[47]

Rabbinic anecdotes, modern Palestinian folk narratives, and Aramaic folk books (the Ahikar novel) have now all been considered. Perhaps it would be advisable to look still further back and examine some familiar Old Testament narratives from the biblical canon. On this subject Theodor Zahn has written a little known but very worthwhile essay entitled "The Historian and His Material in the New Testament." Zahn considers comparative studies to be of great importance because he believes that the basic form of historical description in the New Testament historians did not have to be created de novo. On the contrary, he writes, "The first Christian historians stood between Israel and the Greeks . . . so comparative studies have to bear in mind both Greek and Hebrew historiography."[48]

It is a remarkable and characteristic fact about the Old Testament history books that none of the names of the authors have come down to us. Indeed, the person of the author typically remains quite in the background. An "I" designating the narrator and the main character first appears in late books, such as Ezra and Nehemiah, creating a single whole out of pieces that had previously been narrated in the third person. In earlier historical books, however, and even in late documents like Chronicles and post-canonical 1 Maccabees, there are no references to the person of the author, no introductions, and no personal asides. If by chance some personal color is present, it is only because a prophet was preaching judgment, not because an author was reporting on past events. Belief in the ancient traditions was presupposed throughout, and no need was felt to vouch for the narrative's reliability.

"How different are the Greeks!" Zahn observes. "Distrust of the tradition was part of Greek historiography from the very beginning. It was regarded as an indispensable priority for historians to describe what they themselves had experienced, if not as eyewitnesses, then at least at first hand as contemporaries or

47. A. Schlatter, *Jochanan Ben Zakkai: der Zeitgenosse der Apostel* (1899), 8.
48. Theodor Zahn, "Der Geschichtschreiber und sein Stoff im Neuen Testament," *Zeitschrift für kirchliche Wissenschaft und kirchliches Leben* 9 (1888): 581ff.

from witnesses whose trustworthiness they could control." Thus ἡ ἱστορία is information based on specific investigations and, as far as possible, direct perceptions. In both Thucydides and Polybius, for example, the personality of the historian and his relationship to the events in question stands boldly in the foreground. Herodotus begins his work with his full name, thereby explaining the "I" which immediately follows. Over and over again such historians present us with the "I" or "we" of an investigator or narrator. In later eras of Greek literature this "method" eventually became stylishly deceptive. On the basis of such arguments Zahn arrives at the following conclusion about the gospels: "The author of our first Gospel knew absolutely nothing about the art and form of Greek historiography. It reads like a work of Old Testament history." The same holds true for Mark. In the Gospel of John there is direct address to the reader ("you"), which presupposes an "I" who is speaking, a detail John lacks only in form but not in substance. But "this evangelist was not Greek. He was not the apostle John, but we still don't have to take him for a Greek. Yet he had lived outside of Palestine under the Greeks long enough to know their needs." And what about Luke? "A Greek breeze wafts over Luke. The author frequently steps forward with his 'I.'"

These observations by Zahn are, on the whole, correct and important. His assessment of the Synoptics is certainly right,[49] and his depiction of the fourth evangelist may be questioned, but his method of contrasting Israelite and Greek literature is completely wrong. He makes the same mistake as J. Weiss, who, as we have seen, played off popular Jewish literature against cultivated Greek literature. Zahn's comments about the opposition between Old Testament folk historians and Greek literature completely miss the point of the question about Judaism and Hellenism. For there are Greek documents of which Zahn fails to take note. Gressmann and Dibelius may cite Jewish parallels to the gospels, but they do not think of them as part of a general opposition between Judaism and Hellenism. Rather, they both speak of folk narratives and folk books, thereby emphasizing the concept of the popular, a concept that transcends the question of Judaism and Hellenism.[50]

49. In my opinion, Zahn's remarks here simply cannot be reconciled with his earlier description of the gospels as ἀπομνημονεύματα τῶν ἀποστόλων (cf. above, p. 8–9). In his 1889 essay on the history of the canon, which dealt with Justin's label for the gospels, Zahn placed decisive emphasis on the idea that the evangelists were as reliable in their information about Jesus as Xenophon was about Socrates. But in the 1888 essay that I am describing here, he stresses the opposition between Matthew and Mark, on the one hand (no authorial "I"), and Xenophon, on the other (author = "I"). He refers only in passing to Xenophon's work. At the very least, there is a slight slip in the accent between these two essays.

50. This method lies entirely outside Zahn's field of vision.

3

Low literature from various periods and peoples.

Thus we come back to Greek literature—not to high literature, however, but to low literature, a realm in which many comparisons with the gospels are to be found. Dibelius,[51] for whom the Jewish rabbinic tradition could be an analogy to the gospels only under strict conditions, declares: "The content of the primitive Christian preaching corresponds far more readily to the short stories and didactic 'sententious' sayings of Greek philosophers in specific situations, which were conveyed to a wider public, i.e., to the so-called *chreiai*.[52] Lives of philosophers, and occasionally their diatribes, were stocked with such anecdotes, and books like Lucian's *Demonax* were almost entirely made up of them."[53]

The paradigms of the Gospel tradition are similar to these *chreiai* in that they contain small units, usually with a maxim as the punch line, gathered together for a didactic purpose. They do not stem from great literature. Certainly the sharp style of the *chreiai* (often the punch line is a joke) comes from a world to which the gospels do not belong, and Dibelius rightly sees that difference as the limit beyond which the comparison cannot be drawn. He then makes a topical connection between the novelistic miracle stories of the gospels and contemporary literary miracle narratives.[54] In the Gospel of John he finds "finished literary short stories, whose novelistic form preceded the Fourth Evangelist just as the ancient form of the Apollonius story preceded Philostratus."[55] In the framework of the primitive Christian parenesis, the words of Jesus were eventually brought together with parenetic excerpts from the Pauline letters: "Individual

51. M. Dibelius, *Die Formgeschichte des Evangeliums* (1919), 18. [This material is discussed, in revised and expanded form, on pp. 152–64 of *From Tradition to Gospel*. Trans.]

52. A collection of sayings of Greek philosophers in the *chreia* form is given by G. von Wartensleben, *Begriff der griechischen Chreia und Beiträge zur Geschichte ihrer Form* (1901), 31ff. Cf. also Dibelius, *From Tradition to Gospel*, 152–64.

53. In a footnote, Dibelius draws attention to the formal similarity between John 20:30f. and Lucian, *Demonax* 67. [Schmidt refers here to the footnote in *From Tradition to Gospel*, p. 40, n. 3. Trans.]

54. Dibelius, *From Tradition to Gospel*, 85.

55. Ibid., 91. Cf. also K. L. Schmidt, "Der johanneische Charakter der Erzählung vom Hochzeitswunder in Kana," *Harnack-Ehrung* (1921), 32–43.

admonitions, often in the form of maxims, were loosely strung together or stood disconnected side by side. Other texts which contain parenetic maxims come to mind, such as the first chapter of *James,* the first section of the *Didache, Pseudo-Phocylides, Tobit* 4 and 12, and the corresponding chapter of the Ahikar novel, or Isocrates (*ad Nicoclem*) and Ps. Isocrates (*ad Demonicum*)."[56]

While Dibelius compares individual gospel stories (paradigms and short stories) and sayings collections with corresponding pieces from contemporaneous low literature, Wendland[57] seeks to fit whole gospels into the general history of literature:

> It is the task of an author to create a unified whole out of scattered traditions. We can trace processes of collecting, editing, and compiling oral traditions—i.e., of elevating them to the level of literature—in many geographical regions, and the analogies are highly instructive. The Greeks, for example, collected the stories of Homer and the fables and aphorisms of Aesop. Later editors built on this literary foundation, and such folk books—which are not "literature" in the strict sense of the word—always preserved something of the free movement of the oral tradition. Christian monastic stories (e.g., stories of Egyptian monks or the *Historia Lausiaca*) are of this sort: they are reports from eyewitnesses who traveled to the hermitages and then retold the stories by heart, as they had heard them from the saints' mouths. The size of a work is no indication of the amount of individual influence that is present.[58]

This last comment is especially applicable to Herodotus, who freely fashions the material like an artist but still depends on a popular novelistic tradition: "Artistic creativity and unity is constrained by dependence on traditional material."

Wendland then interprets various units in the gospels in relation to these basic issues. With regard to the characterization (psychology) of the gospels, he asserts: "Mark, like Genesis and Herodotus, avoids direct characterization. The ethos of the person comes out only indirectly, through actions and words. The words are rendered in short direct quotes. Nothing was known of indirect quotation. Ideas are also occasionally quoted, but to the naïve mind, thoughts and words were the same."[59] The style of the Gospel of John is comparable to that of Philostratus's *Apollonius of Tyana.* With regard to later miracle stories (infancy narratives, apocryphal gospels), Wendland writes: "We observe a similar process in hagiography: the reports of reliable eyewitnesses are displaced by collections of miracles written with a more arbitrary interest in local or national

---

56. Dibelius, *From Tradition to Gospel*, 238.

57. P. Wendland, *Die urchristlichen Literaturformen* (1912), 255f., 271, 272, 285, 299, 300, 307.

58. Note the strong disagreement between Wendland and Heinrici; cf. above, p. 4, 6.

59. Cf. the same observation by J. Weiss (above, p. 11), although his evaluation of it is completely different.

saints. The historical picture of these saints fades away as it becomes idealized according to the tastes of a later era." In the Gospel of John, the miracles of Jesus are narrated, and then the signs are discussed; "and in the very same way ancient biographies of miracle workers also made changes, additions, and accentuations, selecting them from a virtually inexhaustible supply (Jn. 20:30; 21:25)."[60] If the tradition of Jesus' words progressively developed to the point where it moved from isolated apophthegmatic units into the formation of clusters, then "the growth and expansion of Cynic literature offers noteworthy analogies: here too we start with a non-literary foundation, followed by records of the teacher in memoir form, collections of striking words and scenes, clusters of pronouncements, and individual thoughts assembled into connected sayings."

At this point Wendland rightly recognizes the limit of such a comparison: "The essential difference is that the authority of the Lord's words gave the Jesus tradition somewhat greater stability." Be that as it may, the essential point to recognize about the gospels lies in their early stages, that is, not in the individuality of the author, but rather in the process of development that preceded the author. Wendland rightly concludes: "We can only understand him (the author) and reconstruct individual cases if historical and philological work go hand in hand as they do in analysis of Homeric poems or the Pentateuch." With all of these folk books, the original tradition is very complicated. "Such texts are heavily worked over, expanded, and distorted. It was no different with the gospels, at least up until canonization, when scholarly effort began to shield the texts to some degree from further proliferation."[61]

I have already mentioned that Dibelius and Gressmann have also pursued this line of investigation, and that Reitzenstein has commented on the Moiragenes material in Philostratus's *Life of Apollonius of Tyana*.[62]

In an essay on miracles in the New Testament, Arnold Meyer[63] relates the gospels to the Hellenistic miracle literature that early Christianity encountered as it propagated and defended its message in literature. Meyer characterizes miracle literature, which comes from "an era when the making of books had no end," as

oral traditions [that] were collected, along with notes, letters, and documents both genuine and falsified . . . Miracle stories were then strung together, and a biography of the miracle-worker was formed, starting with the first miracle and

60. Cf., similarly, Dibelius, above, p. 7n. 15.

61. This observation leads further into textual criticism in the narrower sense. E. von Dobschutz rightly concludes: "The tradition of the New Testament is not at all comparable with the classics or with the church fathers: folk-books are the analogy, e.g., the Alexander novel, the apocryphal acts. Only documents which are close to a tradition can compete with the richness of the New Testament writings" ("Vom Auslegen insonderheit des Neuen Testaments," *Hallische Universitätsreden* 18 [1922]: 24).

62. Cf. above, p. 10.

63. A. Meyer, *Religion in Geschichte und Gegenwart* 5 (1913), 2151ff.

leading to an amazing conclusion after a remarkable series of events, including healings, persecutions, accusations, and imprisonment. Even the birth of the hero was bathed in miraculous light . . . Clever conversations with friends and foes were then added, including pleas of defense before civil magistrates.

This description corresponds to what Meyer says about the gospels: "miracle stories, which originally had a quite different meaning, were linked together on the basis of references to time or place and bound into a biography or travelogue—that is what Mark consists of—then sayings and strings of sayings were interspersed and interpolated—that is what Matthew and Luke consist of—finally, new sayings were created—John!"

Hans von Soden[64] derives the genre "gospel" from Jewish apocalyptic[65] and characterizes it as "highly developed, since it was created by drawing together many dissimilar elements and was influenced by various Jewish and Hellenistic prototypes." He asserts that Luke expanded Mark in the direction of Hellenistic philosophical biography.

As opposed to these studies, W. Bousset thoroughly investigated the textual tradition of the so-called *Apophthegmata Patrum,* because he was convinced that it was analogous to the gospels. Referring to the nonliterary character of the traditional apophthegms, he asserts his "belief in the fact that their value and their charm are completely due to their development from oral tradition—our gospels are comparable."[66]

Likewise H. Lietzmann has studied a text that belongs to the popular monastic literature, Antony's *Life of St. Simeon Stylites:*

The compilation of Antony's *Life* poses a serious challenge, but it richly repays the trouble in that the final outcome is entirely typical of the kinds of constant textual changes which a popular and living tradition can make in written and translated documents. It thus offers a splendid propaedeutic for critical treatment of the Synoptic problem. After working through the textual history of a hagiography like this, one can turn to the gospels and immediately see and correctly assess a large number of both similarities and differences, all of which remain hidden to those who know only the normal traditional forms of high literature. This is why variant texts were communicated with a fullness not justified by their historical worth. I was interested in making this masterpiece of the genre readily accessible.

Rudolf Otto draws attention to similar analogies in both ancient and recent time periods when he recommends "gaining a more tangible perception of living

64. H. von Soden, "Die Entstehung der christlichen Kirche," *Aus Natur und Geisteswelt* 690 (1919): 66ff.

65. Cf. below, p. 25.

66. Wilhelm Bousset, "Die Textüberlieferung der Apophthegmata Patrum," in *Festgabe für A. von Harnack* (1921), 102–16.

and observable examples where original and authentic religious conventicles and communities spring up. We must search for times and places where religion is still alive as a natural, instinctive and naïve driving impulse. More or less tightly organized circles of adherents ensue. 'Sayings,' narratives, and legends are formed and collected." In a footnote Otto adds: "It is surprising that the origin of the Gospel sayings collection, the chief problem of Gospel criticism, has not been studied in this living milieu. And it is even more surprising that the sayings have only recently been related to the highly analogous milieu of the *Apophtheg-mata Patrum,* the *Hadith* of Mohammed, or the Franciscan legends, and particularly the sayings of Rama Krishna, which were collected in our own day."[67]

Otto's suggestions were recently taken up by Wilhelm Michaelis[68] in a short study on the Sadhu tradition and the Jesus tradition. The Sadhu tradition has the advantage of being easy to observe and investigate, and B. H. Streeter of Oxford, along with A. J. Appasamy, published notes on the teachings of Sadhu Sundar Singh that have now appeared in a German translation by P. Baltzer.[69] These two erudite scholars assembled various sources, including previously published works that recorded utterances of the Sadhu in shorthand notes or dictation (English and Tamil). Appasamy, whose mother tongue is Tamil, made notes on various conversations he had during the weeks he spent with the Sadhu in Oxford, London, and Paris. Another person, who also had earlier discussions with the Sadhu, was helpful as well. Thus, when the notes from ancient records and from the conversations were brought together through the careful work of conscientious scholars, the result was a meaningful point of comparison to the Jesus tradition. One could consider whether in a similar manner this or that polemical saying of Jesus might have been cited as an opposing tradition in the broad stream of the tradition. And it is equally significant that when the Sadhu tradition was analyzed by modern methods, it showed properties like those we also find in the gospels. Streeter writes:

> The spirit of the Sadhu is an inexhaustible storehouse of short narratives, examples, epigrams and parables; but he never makes even the slightest effort to avoid repetitions. . . . Over and over we found the same basic ideas in more than one of the written or printed sources we used. 'My mouth,' he says, 'is not dependent on any copyright'—and later we found that many of the sayings which we heard and wrote down as they came from his lips, had already been printed elsewhere. In most cases the readings differ very little from each other, but we gave ourselves the freedom to improve or replace one reading with another, even after the reading seemed suitable to us, and since English is not the Sadhu's mother

67. Rudolf Otto, *Das Heilige,* 8th ed. (1922), 193. [The standard English edition of Otto's classic work, *The Idea of the Holy,* is based on the ninth edition *of Das Heilige,* and does not include this material. Trans.]

68. Wilhelm Michaelis, *Theologische Blätter* (1922), col. 275ff.

69. Under the title "Christian Mysticism in an Indian Soul," with a foreword by the Archbishop of Upssala (Nathan Soderblom), 1922.

tongue, we frequently allowed ourselves to make improvements of a purely ver-
bal character.

Michaelis rightly remarks at this point: "Luke's opening remarks about his
methodology pale in comparison to what conscientious modern scholars know
they are obligated to tell us about their use of sources." In any case, the collectors of the Sadhu tradition, like the collectors of the Jesus tradition, let repeti-
tions stand. The same saying of Jesus—spoken more than once in similar or
different situations—could be handed down with variations in different sources,
or even in the same source. An even more instructive instance from the Sadhu
story is this: reporting on an encounter between someone and the Sadhu, the editors comment that they are not certain whether the Sadhu's answer was given on
this or on some other occasion.

The entire comparison, which Michaelis follows through with these important and correct observations, has a limit that he does not appreciate: the Sadhu
tradition was basically formed from the Sadhu himself or from individual "inter-
locutors," but as far as we can tell, the Jesus tradition was formed by a community. True, the community handed down some sayings of Jesus without alteration.
And even without accepting Papias's supposition about Peter's memoirs, we know
that individuals did form and hand down some sayings of Jesus. But on the
whole, the situation was like that of a folk song, the originator of which is the
people—so much so, in fact, that the individual can be creative only as a representative of the people. The Sadhu tradition is different, but it does have an instructive similarity with the Jesus tradition: they both have at their hub a nonliterary
personality, the essence of which was taken up into a "literary" representation.

The nonliterary beginnings of such "literature" are decisive, and they cannot be effaced by the work of literati. The similarity with the gospels is more significant if the literature has not fully (or only barely) emerged from popular
tradition, as for example if the authorial personality intervened relatively late.

In closing, two opinions that have been expressed more in passing can illustrate that other researchers have also been inclined to understand the gospels
through nonliterary considerations. In a book-length essay on Jesus Christ,
W. Heitmüller wrote this about the character of Mark: "The evangelist reports
just like a naïve folk-narrator; he relates individual narratives (anecdotes), or
groups of them, and he does not mention the time or place of the events."[70] And
A. Jülicher criticizes W. Wrede's work on the Gospel of Mark this way: "Wrede
could have perceived a broader range of psychological possibilities if he had
done wider studies in the history of religions—and not in the same way he has
always done them, i.e., by studying the spiritual heights of Luther, Carlyle, Tolstoy,
et al., but rather in the anonymous literature of the saints and especially in the
production of legends."[71]

70. W. Heitmüller, *Die Religion in Geschichte und Gegenwart* 3 (1912), col. 354.
71. A. Jülicher, *Realenzyklopädie für prot. Theol. und Kirche*, 21.510.

4

ANALOGY, NOT GENEALOGY; GOSPELS AND JEWISH APOCALYPTIC?

All the studies reported on so far have attempted to appreciate the gospels from a literary-historical point of view by means of analogy (the gospels originate *like* writings of another similar genre), and not by means of genealogy (the gospels originate *from* writings of another similar genre). This latter method has now been entertained by Hans von Soden, who would allow that the gospels originated in Jewish apocalyptic. The overall perspective of the gospels betrays its basis in apocalypticism as follows: as in apocalyptic, where a narrative story in futuristic style guarantees that the predictions of the End are correct, so the story of Jesus' life was told as a guarantee of the Christian prediction of the coming Messiah, as part of the prediction that had already been fulfilled. "Thus in Christianity the futuristic form of the apocalypse had to be stripped off, producing a uniquely Christian literary genre: a narrative Gospel with an apocalyptic point."[72]

R. Bultmann would especially like to bring the sayings source Q into relationship with apocalyptic documents like the parenesis of Ethiopian Enoch, since Q also includes parenesis and eschatological predictions and is plainly consistent with an apocalyptic outlook. He does not go along, however (and in my opinion, with good reason), with von Soden's conclusion about the prototype of the gospels:

> In the Christian tradition there is no indication that the life of Jesus was ever narrated in futuristic style. Further, it moved only gradually—beginning with the passion narrative—toward telling the story as a fulfilled prediction. In apocalyptic, the story which precedes the End is not the story of the Messiah but the story of the *aion houtos,* i.e., of the people who are subjected to the sufferings of the present age. Besides, even when the Messiah is introduced as the object of a prediction, he is not allowed to appear on stage to such an extent that he becomes the main character, as is the case in Mark and both of the other Synoptics.[73]

I would like to take this objection a bit further: von Soden is right in saying that our gospels are highly developed creations put together out of many and various

72. von Soden, "Die Entstehung der christlichen Kirche," 66.
73. R. Bultmann, *History of the Synoptic Tradition,* trans. John Marsh (1921), 228, 510.

elements and that many different Jewish and Hellenistic influences contributed to their development. But I believe that this multiplicity and multiformity inhere from the very beginning in the individual constituent parts of the gospels, and thus that there is no possibility of extracting an original gospel with a basic apocalyptic scheme.

PART TWO

THE PLACE OF THE GOSPELS IN THE GENERAL HISTORY OF LITERATURE

If we look elsewhere to find the literary germ of the gospels—and if one can be recovered, late Jewish apocalyptic is actually a distinct possibility[1]—we must basically consider only analogies to the gospels. In our critical review of earlier studies, we repeatedly ran into one fact that proves that analogy is the only sensible and productive method, and now we must take full advantage of all its ramifications: *a Gospel is by nature not high literature, but low literature; not the product of an individual author, but a folk-book; not a biography, but a cult legend.* Faint hints to the contrary do not change the total picture in the slightest. Luke may well have possessed the skills of an author, but he could not and would not have produced a biography of Jesus. Even the Fourth Gospel—which is personal confession of a sort—has more tradition behind it than we could ever ascertain. Above and beyond its personal aspects, it is the product of a confessing community. The gospels do not belong to any specific strand in the history of literature, and despite their borrowings from "the world," neither do their non-canonical offshoots, since the earlier gospels always remained their prototype.

1. H. Jordan, *Geschichte der altchristlichen Literatur* (1911), 73n. 1: "It is certain that the historiography of the Gospels is dependent on Jewish-Israelite conceptions of history. Apocalyptic was particularly influential. But I do not think that strong threads run from Israelite historiography in the Old Testament, or Jewish historiography in the Apocrypha (cf. Maccabees) to the general form of the Gospels." This conclusion is probably right, but Jordan does not state the grounds for it.

1

The Literary Development of the Noncanonical Acts, (Literary) Lives of Saints, and Martyr-Acts; the Passion Narrative of Jesus; Gospels and the Formation of the Canon.

The apocryphal acts, by contrast, do follow definite literary rules and do belong in the history of the Hellenistic novel.[2] It has already been clearly shown that some lives of saints have to be explained—genealogically—from the history of Greek literature. Thus, K. Holl has demonstrated that the second type of martyr acts, the trial transcripts, must have a literary derivation: "It may be regarded as established that Christian trial narratives are related to a Hellenistic literary genre which was already widely developed in the second century CE."[3] (The first type, the narrative letter, does not preclude authorial intent and stems from Jewish antecedents.)

An important shift of content took place. As enthusiasm waned during the age of the apologists, the early Christian idea of a martyr-prophet was gradually displaced by more philosophical conceptions of martyrdom. "The world" exerted its influence: both Greek philosophers and Roman heroes served as exemplars. Even more significantly, this literary genre was formed as the apologists' theology "introduced into Christianity a new standard for authenticity." Thus, the structure of the trial transcripts increasingly emphasized the oratorical skill of the martyr. Detailed speeches were produced, as in the Hellenistic prototypes. Historians should not be overly skeptical at this point, since it can be assumed that some martyrs actually did make rather long speeches and that in many cases local Christian communities did possess official trial records. But on the whole, the trial acts are an art form, one that eventually displaced the narrative letter as it steadily developed in a literary direction. The "transcript" grew into a dramatic construction. Indeed, as monks—whom the church regarded as saints—approached the status of martyrs, this dramatic construction came to have the sense of a life of the saint, bringing his or her inner experiences out into

2. Cf. in this regard E. von Dobschütz, "Der Roman in der altchristlichen Literatur," *Deutsche Revue* 3 (1902), 87ff.

3. K. Holl, "Die Vorstellung vom Märtyrer und die Märtyrerakten in ihrer geschichtlichen Entwicklung," *Neue Jahrbücher für das klassische Altertum* (1914): 521ff.

the open. In some cases this effort actually paid more attention to the early life of the martyr, and the "speeches" receded into the background.

The martyr acts arouse particular interest because the passion narrative of Jesus is, in content at least, a martyr story. Comparison with the martyr acts is also suggested by the fact that the passion narrative is an account more or less complete in and of itself—as opposed to the rest of the stock of gospel narratives—an account that shows only a few seams and grooves and thus has to be evaluated as literature.[4] As we have seen, in the early Christian martyr acts the trial transcript constituted its own genre, but only very faint beginnings in this direction can be detected in the passion narrative of Jesus. Something like a trial transcript lies behind Jesus' appearance before Annas in the Fourth Gospel, and the Gospel of Matthew (27:2, 11) highlights the official position of Pilate. On the other hand, the passion narrative of Jesus takes little interest in the person of Pilate the judge, whereas in the trial transcripts the judge stands in the foreground. All of this shows that the passion of Jesus, as it now stands in the gospels, does not hark back to any literary genre but is based instead on living, popular, cultic tradition. It also explains why Jesus has so remarkably little to say—indeed, he is almost completely silent. If, in a similar way, some of the Christian and pagan martyr acts lack a strong emphasis on the martyr's words, they approach the gospel passion narrative and distance themselves from the genre of the trial transcripts.[5]

A literary history like this, which both indirectly and directly relates the apocryphal acts, the lives of the saints, and especially the martyr acts to the general history of literature, is simply out of the question for the gospels. Why? Why weren't the gospels involved in secular literary history? It is worth considering that the formation of the canon may have cut short any possible development in that direction. The apologist Justin, who had a taste for authenticating and verifying earliest Christianity, had the chance to change the gospels, making them more "authentic." He adduced documentation for both the miracles of Jesus and for the proceedings of the crucifixion by referring to the *Acts of Pilate* (*First Apology* 48.3, 35.9), and he documented the birth in Bethlehem by referring to the registers from the census of Quirinius (*First Apology* 34.2). Such documentation may have represented itself as historical, but this device actually served to make the gospels less historical and more literary. For these "documents" did not exist; Justin, at any rate, had never laid eyes on them. Fortunately, the gospels were allowed to be what they were, and the story of Jesus was written without source references. Justin was the only one to call the gospels ἀπομνημονεύματα

---

4. Cf. my book, *Der Rahmen der Geschichte Jesu* (1919), 303ff.; M. Dibelius, *Die Formgeschichte des Evangeliums* (1919). R. Bultmann sees it slightly differently, *The History of the Synoptic Tradition* (1921); see also G. Bertram, *Die Leidensgeschichte Jesu und der Christuskult* (1922).

5. U. Wilcken draws attention to this criterion (i.e., the length of the speeches) in his paper, "Zum alexandrinischen Antisemitismus," *Abhandlungen der Sächs. Gesellschaft der Wissenschaften* (1909), 837.

τῶν ἀποστόλων, and even he could do no more than give them a title that emphasized their authenticity.

In addition to the fact that canonization hindered the gospels' literary development, it seems to me that the following observation is also significant: from the very beginning, the gospels had a peculiar character that, as we have noted again and again, was resistant to literary evolution and development. Many lives of saints had this same quality, and even the martyr acts could not fit completely into literary history; but with the gospels, this is true to an even greater extent. And even though it is very difficult to know exactly what would have happened to the gospels if the canon had not been formed, it can still be said with confidence that because of their peculiar mass and proportion, the gospels would have remained what they were, no matter what. The formation of the canon simply gave external polish to a quality that was already finished on the inside.

2

GOSPELS AND BIOGRAPHY: ARRANGEMENT OF THE MATERIAL, PORTRAITURE, THE PROBLEM OF TRUTH-CONTENT.

This discussion shows that the gospels were not drawn into the kind of literary development that we can observe among the apocryphal acts, lives of saints, and martyr acts. This indirect line of reasoning can now be expanded directly to the view that the only possible genre left with which to classify the gospels is biography. Our earlier arguments have already demonstrated the sterility of the idea that the gospels are comparable to Greek biographies and memoirs, but do the gospels hark back to biography at all? That depends on how the concept of biography is defined. A glance at various handbooks and technical introductions shows just how difficult this can be.[6] A full-fledged biography employs the techniques of narrative art to describe the life of a person, including both inward and outward development. To that end, questions about the order of the material (sequences of content and chronology), pragmatics, psychology, characterization, and portraiture[7] are of decisive importance. The gospels are almost entirely devoid of such things. By contrast, it is significant that the apocryphal acts, which were included in Greek literary development, have all sorts of prosopographical finery, including thorough physical descriptions like the one given of Paul in *The Acts of Paul and Thecla* 2. The gospels and the canonical Acts have nothing of the kind.

Although ancient biography may have been different from modern, it did have an essential interest in portraiture. The same is true of the special genre of ἐγκώμιον and of peripatetic biography with its indirect characterization. As the Alexandrian philologists of Kallimachus's and Eratosthenes' generation took up the task of chronological and biographical research, Greece experienced a rich historical and literary output that focused on the observation and description of personalities. Arrangement of the material was more important than characterization, as Suetonius' biographies of the Caesars aptly illustrate. In the *Vita*

---

6. E. Bernheim, *Lehrbuch der historischen Methode und der Geschichtsphilosophie* (1908).

7. For antiquity, cf. I. Bruns, *Das literarische Porträt der Griechen im 5. und 4. Jahrhundert* (1896); further, I. Fürst, *Die literarische Porträtmanier im Bereich des griechisch-römischen Schrifttums* (1902).

Augusti, for example, the opening chapters follow a chronological order, but there follows an explanation that the contents should properly be recounted, not in continuous narrative but in excerpts, not chronologically but in a practical arrangement. In this biography a well-defined scheme is vigorously carried through from start to finish. It may be asked whether this kind of clear methodology may not be foundational to the concept of biography. Some like to speak of "biography" even when these features are lacking, but in such cases it is better to introduce a new concept, perhaps that of folk biography, that is, popular biography. In any event, the essential thing is never to lose sight of the marks of low literature, of a folk book.

Unfortunately this issue of Gospel studies that so interests us has repeatedly gotten bogged down in questions about historical truth. There is one obvious reason why Papias and especially Justin still find a following in their efforts to verify and authenticate the gospel material and thereby to include the gospels in Greek memoir literature: it is the basic assumption that a real biography, because it is high literature, the product of an individual literary author, offers a better guarantee of historical factuality than low literature, which is mere cult legend and popular depiction. In many cases, this assumption is justified. Biography from the pen of a modern historian *is* more reliable than a folk book. In antiquity, however, that was not necessarily the case. For there was no hard-and-fast distinction between historiography and rhetoric. The historiographer stood, as it were, in the middle between the rhetor and the poet.[8] It may look like frills to us, but to the ancients it was very nearly the most important point: their historians strove for literary polish above all else, and if need be, they were less concerned about historical truth. Under these circumstances low literature, which has no literary pretensions, can be of more historical value than high literature, which does.

8. E. Norden, *Die antike Kunstprosa* (1898), 81ff.

3

THE BOUNDARY BETWEEN HIGH LITERATURE AND LOW LITERATURE: THE GOSPELS AND PHILOSTRATUS' *LIFE OF APOLLONIUS OF TYANA.*

Even though (as has already been mentioned) the boundary between artistic literature and a folk book is not always easy to trace, that boundary is nonetheless relevant to our discussion of recurrent efforts to fit the gospels into ancient biographical literature. It shows that the mere absence of chronological construction and psychological development (which is in many ways characteristic of biographical literature) must not be confused with the gospels' lack of interest in these same points: an inferior product cannot be compared with a natural growth. In the Hellenistic era countless authors, peripatetics for the most part, wrote βίοι of ancient poets and sages, often taking the folk book of Homer's life as something of a model.[9] The boundary line I am referring to is thus not easy to ascertain, but that does not make it irrelevant. Apophthegms and *chreiai* may have flowed into these documents, but that does not make them prototypes of the evangelists, who could not and would not engage in periodization or psychologization.

The situation would be different if, instead of taking up only individual popular pieces, which do not affect the overall character of his authorial work, an author took up a whole complex of such pieces, which would stamp its imprint on the entire product. This is in fact what happened in the case of Philostratus's *Life of Apollonius of Tyana,* which fits particularly well with the gospels. Philostratus, who intends to narrate the life (βίοι, I.9) of Apollonius, is a true man of letters with a definite literary purpose. His skillful treatment of ὑπομνήματα represents a rhetorization of the grammatical βίοι. Like Plutarch and other biographers, he wants to present the public with a well-written book, and an authorial "I" runs all the way through it. The plan and form of the entire work is laid out in detail at the beginning (I.2, 3); written sources and oral tradition are to be used. The author's task, then, is not only to present the material in full but to do so in good style.

Philostratus blames one predecessor (Moiragenes) for the incompleteness of the material (there was so much Moiragenes did not know), and another (Damis) for the lack of style (he expressed himself clearly but with no skill at

9. V. Wilamowitz-Möllendorf, *Die Kultur der Gegenwart* I.8.2 (1907), 118.

all). But is that what really happened? Recently there have been doubts about whether Philostratus ever actually used any written sources. According to Eduard Meyer,[10] he produced most of the material himself, particularly Damis's ὑπομνήματα which receive so much attention, and he would have been astonished to find that anyone actually believed Damis was real. It was all simply stylish packaging in the manner of the Second Sophistic: an educated man of letters is interested in any and all kinds of information. In order to change the picture of Apollonius given by the tradition, Philostratus invented his written sources as part of a latent polemic against Moiragenes. He produced Damis and also Maximus, who authenticated the chronology of events in the Aegean, as well as letters of Apollonius, and more. If Eduard Meyer is right, there can be no comparison with the gospels at all:[11] a "manufactured" novel is the exact opposite of a growing gospel tradition. Comparisons with the Gospel of Luke also inevitably shrivel up, since a bogus pretense (Eduard Meyer vents every ounce of his displeasure at Philostratus) is something quite different from an honest work like Luke.

In my opinion, Philostratus actually did leave a very strong imprint on the material he passed on (for just this reason he is to be assessed completely differently from the evangelists, even Luke and the fourth evangelist). Much of it strikes the reader as fictitious. The Damis pieces were at least partially invented, as were a number of letters supposedly written by Apollonius. Yet in all frankness, this matter must be addressed in two parts: (1) Philostratus's need and capacity for fiction show definite limits. Distinctions have to be drawn between "Damis" (probably a pseudonym) and Philostratus. The crass miracle stories, which are the principal difficulty for Eduard Meyer, could equally well have been told by a contemporary of Apollonius. There are plenty of parallels for that kind of thing in the realm of folk books and lives of saints. (2) It is important to get a clear idea of Philostratus's method of working, but we must not neglect to circumscribe the peculiarity of the tradition in very bold strokes.[12] That means going into the history of this tradition, a tradition that had anonymous origins prior to, and independent of, the author's personality. With regard to the work of "Damis," notice that the sketch of the prophet's debut, that is, when he attracts his first disciples, says nothing about his age. Indeed, it offers so little in the way of chronology that it is hard to determine how long a time period should be assigned to this relatively small amount of material. Short, frequently obscure sayings form the kernel around which the narrative is gathered. On the whole it has to be assumed that "Damis" and the other pieces already had a history behind them going back to traditions close to the historical Apollonius.

10. E. Meyer, "Apollonios von Tyana und Philostratos," *Hermes* (1917): 371–424.

11. It used to be popular to assume that Philostratus intentionally created his work as a parallel to the gospels, but today that hypothesis is almost completely rejected, and with good reason.

12. Eduard Meyer does not understand this task because his methodology for studying the gospels is the exact opposite of a form-critical method.

At this point it becomes difficult to avoid comparisons with the gospels. Philostratus the author may not be comparable to the evangelists, but that dear old comparison still has some validity, since the preliminary stages of the *Life of Apollonius* correspond to the preliminary stages of the gospels, and even to the gospels themselves. In both cases individual units of tradition of various origins and forms have grown together. This is the only way to explain the undeniable similarities in composition and in some individual units. Individual stories and traditions lie behind Philostratus and his sources; rightly understood, they (like the gospels) lead us back to a popular, nonliterary type of narration.

4

Simple Cases of Folk Biography: *Littérature Orale.*

The preceding discussion makes it clear that direct comparisons between the gospels and the Apollonius tradition are essentially and ultimately meaningless. Although it certainly is tempting to make comparative use of material from the same time period, the same language, and, in a certain sense, even the same content, at bottom nothing really comes of it. For the kind of biographical tradition we are dealing with here follows the same laws of tradition in every era and every language and in every culture, race, and creed. In essence it has *no time or place,* nor is it conditioned by the circumstances that created its special literary form.

Where do we find material that is comparable to the gospels? This question can be answered very quickly and easily, and the answer lies along the lines already laid down for the relation between Israelite-Jewish and Greek-Hellenistic parallels. From this point forward, the field in which we must look for illustrative parallels can and must be opened as widely as we can imagine. In the selections that follow, I seek to build upon these secure principles. On the whole, I will offer new material that may seem somewhat random, but that is unavoidable because, in the comparative method that I will demonstrate, the content and particular provenance of the parallels are not essential. It is the *form* of the pieces that matters most—pieces that come from different times and different places but that all have to do with popular collections of words and deeds, sayings and stories. "Such folk-books, which are not literary in the strict sense of the word, always preserve something of the free movement of the oral tradition."[13] And the original singularity of oral tradition is the brief individual report.

Very simple cases offer the best illustrations of this point. A rich storehouse of examples can be found in an approximately fifty–volume collection published in Paris under the title, *Les littératures populaires de toutes les nations.* In the first volume, appropriately entitled *Littérature orale de la Haute-Bretagne* (1881), Paul Sébillot observes the forms of individual stories and the collections that arise from them. About this *Littérature orale* he correctly remarks: "One could almost say that it is from every place and from no place."

13. P. Wendland's remark, which I have already quoted above, is confirmed at every turn.

A basic characteristic of oral tradition is that it takes the form of variations, many of which can stand side by side in the same narrative, showing just how unimportant the "connections" are. On the whole, in fact, the connections are quite secondary. The links between individual units are loose and weak, and they provide no basis for either chronology or psychology. The framework in which the stories are set is so weak that sometimes a link is given, and sometimes it is not. Most of the time that is entirely acceptable. Again and again we read, "the next day . . . after that . . . a little later . . . a few days later . . . around the same time . . . another time," and so on. Obviously such indicators do not give the exact time at which events took place. In many cases, stories can be freely substituted for each other in the sequence. Once in a while there may be individual units that do belong together, but in that case the "connection" is based on internal congruity, which is also—properly speaking—secondary. There are no psychological connections, either. Actual physical descriptions are not given; instead, action and speech focus all the attention on the main character, while bystanders fade into the background.

This narrative style is rich in its parsimony, and it usually does not signify an improvement when this quality begins to disappear. New place designations and characters, which either were not in, or are different from, those in the original edition, can appear out of nowhere in later editions and even in the final redaction. Such things come and go, but the motley picture that results does not worry the scholar who can recognize that such designations are simply vague. Editors and commentators on both ancient and modern folk narratives have seen this. As F. M. Luzel, who edited the collection I mentioned above, *Légendes chrétiennes de la Basse-Bretagne,* has aptly put it: "Popular storytellers have a regrettable habit of introducing into their stories names of people and places they know, substituting them for other older names it would be interesting for us to know." And regarding the chronology of these groups of stories, E. Amélineau writes in "*Monuments pour servir à l'histoire de l'Égypte chrétienne au I'V^e et Ve siècles*" (1888):

> I must tell the reader about several distinctive features in the Egyptian style of composition. Over and over in Coptic texts, and in ancient hieroglyphic and hieratic texts, we find expressions like these: "many days after that . . . much later," and so on. Statements like these mean absolutely nothing, or mean simply "the next day." Egyptian storytellers generally attach no significance to precise notions of time; these stock phrases rolled gently off the tongue, and that was all that was needed. They served as vague expressions, as we would commonly say, "*and then*" or "*after that.*" Chronological reconstructions cannot be built on this kind of data.

It is no different with Egyptian folk narratives such as those published by G. Maspero or W. M. Flinders Petrie.

5

Methodology: literary criticism and style criticism (form criticism).

Large portions of the Old and New Testaments also have to be considered. The relevance of this material not been recognized until recently, primarily because of the doctrine of the inspiration of the Bible. If inspiration is taken as the starting point, then emphasis falls upon things that appear to be chronological or psychological but that prove to be vague and unproductive. It is significant that early Protestant biblical scholars were more adamant about inspiration than Catholic scholars of any era. Catholics reproach Protestants for their exaggerated concept of inspiration, which prevents them from rightly recognizing the loose structure of the gospels.[14] In more recent Protestant critical theology and its concomitant philology, the doctrine of inspiration has transformed itself into an oddly doctrinaire ideology of a "people of the book." It searches for an Ur-Gospel that is complete in itself and that is consistent both psychologically and chronologically, and it pursues a penetrating literary criticism, all of which leads to a downright bizarre result: the document at the bottom of the synoptic tradition turns out to be found, not in Mark or even Ur-Mark, but in Luke.[15] Traditionally-minded scholars like Theodor Zahn are being just as rigid when they base arguments on the outline of the Gospel of John. In both cases, things are being emphasized that simply will not bear that emphasis.

In the field of Old Testament studies, H. Gunkel's work on genre has produced a telling attack on the rigid and overworked literary criticism of Wellhausen and his pupils. This is not the place to explore how far it is possible or necessary to do further literary-critical work on the Pentateuch, the basic principles of which are now quite secure,[16] but Gunkel's commentary on Genesis has certainly had the lasting benefit of calling biblical scholars' attention to the investigation of the literary forms of the documents, especially their components. There

14. For particular instances, see my book, *Der Rahmen der Geschichte Jesu*, 10f.
15. F. Spitta, *Die synoptische Grundschrift in ihrer Überlieferung durch das Lukas-Evangelium* (1912).
16. I prefer to say "possibility" rather than "necessity." O. Eissfeldt reaches the opposite conclusion in his essay, "Zum gegenwärtigen Stand der Pentateuch-kritik," *Zeitschrift für Missionstunde und Religionswissenschaft* (1919): 113ff., and in his *Hexateuch-Synopse* (1922). He has important differences of opinion here with H. Gunkel and H. Gressmann.

can be no doubt that, as Gunkel has shown, many Old Testament narratives belong in the realm of folk literature. Genesis is "the written record of a popular oral tradition." Gunkel's work on individual pieces, especially the opening paragraphs, corresponds fully with the conclusions I have reached above in relation to both older and more recent folk narratives. The fact of variations, for example, is thrown into sharp relief. "By their very nature popular legends exist in the form of individual stories." But in many cases "the 'connections' between the individual stories originate later." "Narrators of legends do not ask their listeners (as modern novelists can) to be interested in many characters at the same time." "The brevity with which secondary characters are treated is striking. We are accustomed to modern works in which virtually every character who steps on stage is described as an individual in his own right, even if only in outline. Narrators of ancient legends behave quite differently." "By our standards even the portrayal of the main character is remarkably sparing."[17]

Gunkel's remarks capture in writing the very essence of folk narratives, just as we have already learned to recognize it in other settings. What he says about character depiction in particular recalls our earlier investigations of literary "portraiture." A not insignificant methodological detail should be remarked upon here: Gunkel compares and contrasts ancient folk narrators and modern writers respectively. This opposition is certainly illuminating and instructive, but it must be added that (as Gunkel himself knew and even hinted at) the "special popular view of people, which is so pronounced in Genesis,"[18] appears not only in antiquity but also in other eras; it is not unique to antiquity, but is common to all primitive peoples. Gunkel's basic results are not affected by this fact. He insists that the place to begin is with observation of the "individual units" of Genesis. "The most important question is which of these individual units is to receive the most consideration, i.e., which of the different units in the oral tradition is the original? It is a question which recurs in many similar instances: which is the controlling unit: the songbook, the individual collection therein, or the individual song? the Gospel, the sermon, or the individual traditional saying of Jesus? the entire Apocalypse, the separate apocalyptic sources, or the individual visions?"[19]

In this regard, it has rightly been noticed that the question of the gospels, and especially of the Synoptic Problem, ultimately boils down to the question of the "history of the synoptic tradition" or the question of "tradition and composition"[20] in the gospels. Wellhausen's proposals have already taken aim at the earlier stages of the gospels. W. Bousset drew attention to the need for style criticism

17. H. Gunkel, *Genesis,* trans. Mark E. Biddle (Macon, Ga.: Mercer Univ. Press, 1997), xxvii–xxxiii.
18. Ibid., xxxiii.
19. Ibid., xxvii.
20. Cf. my essay, "Der geschichtliche Wert des lukanischen Aufrisses der Geschichte Jesu, Tradition und Komposition im Lukas-Evangelium," *Theologische Studien und Kritiken* (1918).

of the gospels in the first edition of his *Kyrios Christos* (1913), when he dropped a hint that was taken up in the second edition of that great work (1921): "A whole new method needs to be put in place here, one which proceeds with style-criticism and concentrates on studying the laws of oral tradition."[21] The innovative "form-critical" method for studying the gospels puts that plan to work in detail. It proves that with regard to the peculiarity of the gospel tradition, the decisive point is surely not the simple recognition of the Two-Source or the Marcan or some Ur-Marcan hypothesis. It is much more a matter of going behind the sources. As this task is increasingly understood and carried out, it matters less and less whether we can know exactly where Mark found some piece of the tradition. No doubt Gunkel's outlook, especially as it is expressed in the introduction to his commentary on Genesis, has had very fruitful effects. Certainly Dibelius (*From Tradition to Gospel*) and Bultmann (*The History of the Synoptic Tradition*) emphasize their debt to Gunkel. This point has been made over and over again in reviews of their works and of my book, *Der Rahmen der Geschichte Jesu*. Perhaps it could be asserted that this new methodology simply had to succeed, since it was (so to speak) in the air,[22] but that objection does not change the fact that Gunkel was the first and most vigorous advocate for a method that was destined to become widely accepted.

It is more important to answer the question of why this method could be said to have been "in the air." Unlike literary criticism, form criticism does not ask so much about the person who wrote this or that source document, but it speaks instead of the *communities* out of whose common life the early Christian documents, especially the gospels, were formed. An individualistic perspective is exchanged for a more sociological one. Even scholars are products of their time; that is their fate—or their good fortune. Once we notice that even in scientific activity one generation takes over for another, a new approach to the philosophy of history begins to take shape. It is conceivable that a statement of this sort, which sounds so much like a confession, could be used either to resist a new method or to represent it as dangerous or unproductive. That is all the more reason why it must be pointed out that on this point the course of scholarship concurs with the results of work in the history of religions. In both the history and the literature of religion, for that matter, the collective—the community—has acquired more significance than was formerly recognized. Thus, the material and the method stand shoulder to shoulder.

21. Cf. my introduction to the 4th edition (1922) of Bousset's *Kyrios Christos* about Jesus.

22. So likewise M. Albertz in his form-critical work, *Die synoptischen Streitgespräche* (1921); whereas H. Windisch (cf. above) expresses himself as follows: "New Testament scholarship has put these stimuli [Gunkel's] to use, or better, has intensified their impact and occupied itself more comprehensively with these questions." Windisch draws attention to Deissmann, Heinrici, P. Wendland, and J. Weiss, but he does not always arrange them in the correct order of priority.

A. von Harnack made the distinct personalities of the church fathers come vividly to life, and Eduard Meyer did the same for the ancient historians. But a different kind of treatment is called for when it comes to the many anonymous men and women of primitive Christianity, who are lost in the thick darkness of a richly creative era during which creators and founders cannot always be identified precisely. It is symptomatic that von Harnack and Meyer explicitly anchored their studies of gospel literature in the treatment of the Lukan writings. For them Luke was a man cut from the same cloth as Eusebius or Polybius. Even if that were correct—or even if it were only an exaggeration—it would still miss the essential nature of gospel literature. It is the study of the earliest evangelist, Mark, and of the pre-gospel materials, that is decisive. There is a gap between them and Luke, a gap about which there is much more to be said.

It is precisely when we notice the distinctive place of the third evangelist that we can start to have a clear eye for the gospels in general and for their preliminary stages in particular. What I said earlier about the peculiarity of folk narratives, as they have been collected from the Hebrew book of Genesis on down through time, holds equally true for the gospels. In both cases the same issues are at stake: variants, whether chronological and psychological connections are significant, how the original short units are tied together, the treatment of the main character and the secondary characters. My detailed investigations in *Der Rahmen der Geschichte Jesu* stand up to the test of comparisons with these analogies. In the index, the cases I observed are gathered under the following headings: doublets, later (nonhistorical) localization, periodization of events by Luke, psychologization of events by Luke, introductions to pericopes (expressions like δι' ἡμερῶν, ἐν ἐκείνῃ τῇ ἡμέρᾳ, ἐν ἐκείνῳ τῷ καιρῷ, μετὰ ταῦτα, πάλιν, and so on have the same generalizing character that we recognized above), treatment of characters, and Jesus pericopes.

6

THE MULTIFORMITY OF THE FRAMEWORK OF THE STORY OF JESUS; *CHREIA*-TRADITIONS.

There are other things in the gospels, however, that are not covered by the generalizations in the previous chapter, including internal and external connections, and the placement of an individual story or of a particular saying. How should features like these be assessed? In *Der Rahmen der Geschichte Jesu,* I regarded them almost without exception as secondary, as later redactional trimming that must be discarded. This view is correct, at least to the extent that the foundation of the gospels is not, properly speaking, the story of Jesus, but rather *stories* of Jesus. If the evangelists, particularly Luke, were trying to organize and use the rubble of situational indicators so as to produce a continuous readable narrative, their efforts must be regarded as an utter failure. In the case of Mark and Matthew, it is questionable whether they ever seriously entertained the idea of the kind of effort that proponents of an exaggerated Marcan hypothesis believe was successful. But it does not necessarily follow that all the specific details in the framework are secondary and thus historically worthless.

Sweeping generalizations have to be rejected here, not for apologetic reasons (as if to rescue at least a few pieces of the tradition), but rather because of an insight into the form of the situational details. Many of them are so personal and at the same time so vague that they must be regarded as original primitive tradition.[23] If all of these details were formed later when the separate pieces were put together, then the overall outline of the gospels ought to have turned out to be more unified; that is, the particular designations of place, time, and situation should have all had the same character. But the parts of the framework are *never* emphasized. On the one hand, that is precisely what makes them so unproductive; but on the other hand, there is a sense in which they are quite productive.

Collections of *chreiai* can be especially instructive here. *Chreiai*—short stories that culminate in a specific point—naturally have situational details that often make the message of the story, the "punch line," comprehensible. But they also often provide information that is unnecessary, including designations of place or time. If such anecdotes are ever collected (say those concerning a well-known person), something like an outline will result. The anecdotes about Frederick the

---

23. On this point I differentiate myself from Bultmann. See, for example, in his book and mine, the treatment of the situational details in the story of Peter's confession at Caesarea Philippi.

Great, edited and prefaced by Friedrich Nikolai, illustrate this point very nicely. The temporal designations that appear in these stories run the full gamut: sometimes they are completely missing; sometimes they are general (e.g., "once" or "during the Seven Years' War"); sometimes the year, the month, or the day is given. Designations of place run the gamut as well, with an occasional short summary statement at the beginning of an anecdote. Since everything in each anecdote relates to the point of that specific anecdote, there are no real connections in the collection. The enumeration of the years shows plainly that there are no chronological threads. That only happens when two anecdotes of similar content are placed side by side because of their inner relationship.

The analogy with the gospel tradition is obvious. Not only Matthew but also Mark joined together words and deeds of Jesus on the basis of their content. Even where details about his itinerary do appear, it always has to be asked whether the order is a matter of chronology or content. The three stories in Mark 4:35–5:43 (the storm at sea, the Gerasene demoniac, Jairus's daughter, and the woman with an issue of blood) are a good example. At first glance, there appears to be a logical itinerary here, but on closer inspection, the "itinerary" turns out to be hopelessly tangled. Three stories from around the Sea of Galilee, which may have taken place in different years, have been grouped together here. In the gospels and in the analogous collections of *chreiai,* then, sometimes the pictures are framed, and sometimes they are not. Since the collectors of these pieces did not emphasize the framing, they did not change it much, and this accounts for the variety of the situational details.

7

GERMAN FOLK BOOKS: *DOKTOR FAUST.*

As much as a consideration of folk narratives and *chreiai* does allow us to learn about the study of the gospels, it still leaves a good deal unexplained, for the process by which the gospels evolved and split into their present collected editions (the four gospels) is still very difficult to trace. It is advisable, therefore, to bring into the comparison a larger collection of stories, one in which an abundance of traditions has coalesced and then gone out into the world in different versions. The most instructive examples here are the German folk books of *Till Eulenspiegel* and *Doktor Faust*. The latter, to which we will confine ourselves here, passed through several preliminary stages before it was printed for the first time, and its story did not come to an end with that printing: new versions continued to arise, dependent in varying degrees on the first one. This situation (i.e., preliminary stages followed by new versions) corresponds exactly with that of the gospels: Mark, the oldest evangelist, put together a story out of the traditions he had collected, and then his gospel had its own story as it was brought together with newly arriving traditions in the other gospels. In both cases the study of the preliminary stages is beset by special difficulties and hypotheses. By contrast, the study of the early editions is, in the case of the Faust book at least, more certain, because here we are working in an era of printed books and definite dates of publication, and thus questions about dependency among editions can be settled thoroughly and exactly. On the whole, questions of tradition and composition can be answered with greater certainty for a Faust-book than for the gospels.

Even a cursory reading of any old or recent Faust-book (more on the different versions later) quickly shows that we have, not a freely creative narrator or specific authorial personality, but collections of old traditional stories whose form was only somewhat—and never very deeply—affected by the collector. Scholarly studies have confirmed this impression many times over. The peculiar quality of folk narrative, as it was originally deposited in the oral tradition, could not be effaced by any published Faust-book.[24] The extent of this peculiarity is almost always the same, even though various writers have shaped the Faust story, just as Luke (despite the literary pretense of his introduction and presentation of

---

24. Faligan, *Histoire de la légende de Faust* (1888), iv: "The Faust legends were a popular legend, no doubt changed in many respects by the writers who collected them, but born of the oral tradition, whose general appearance and characteristic traits they still retain."

the material) does not differ sharply from the other Synoptics. At present several different local traditions about Faust[25] can be identified: Oberrhein, Wittenberg, Erfurt, Leipzig, Ingolstadt, and Nürnberg. The memory of his practical jokes was particularly lively among younger academics in Erfurt, leading to a local tradition that would eventually be put down in writing. Some lines going back to the Erfurt tradition may have been written down in a chronicle around the middle of the sixteenth century, but it has been argued that this chronicle actually borrowed its stories from the Faust-book and did not come into existence until later.[26] There were also traditions from Leipzig, where all sorts of records about Faust circulated, some true, some false. Later on, stories from Ingolstadt and Nürnberg flowed in as well. Two of these Nürnberg stories were published in a short and in a long version.[27] We thus arrive at a luxuriant growth of tradition that started developing even in the "magician's" own lifetime and became steadily more diverse thereafter. In particular, all kinds of stories about Faust's death got tangled up together. To this assemblage, which already had an ending, there only needed to be added a beginning, and the framework for a biographical folk book was complete: a colorful mix of material was strung together in a loose framework. It remained only to collect it all and bring it under one unified interpretive concept.

The kind of composition that went into the Faust-book becomes evident in the older extant versions of the story (1587 and later: the various editions by Spiess and the Wolfenbüttel version before that) and their expansion by Widman (1599), who inflated the material tremendously. A synoptic survey produces the following "literary critical" results:[28]

W = the Wolfenbüttel version
H = the various editions by Spiess (1587ff)
    A = first edition
    B = a new edition, supposedly from the year 1587 but in reality a
         revision with eight new pranks that stem from books of magic[29]
    C = the version to which the Erfurt chapters were added
    D = a text that combines A and C, printed in Berlin in 1590
Wi = Widman.

---

25. For what follows, see W. Scherer in the foreword to his facsimile of the oldest Faust book (1884); cf. further R. Petsch, *Das Volksbuch vom Doktor Faust nach der ersten Ausgabe 1587* (1911).

26. S. Szamotolski, *Euphorion* 2 (1895), 39ff.

27. Cf. W. Meyer, *Nürnberger Faust-Geschichten* (1895).

28. See R. Petsch, *Das Volksbuch vom Doktor Faust*, xviiiff.

29. Spiess's trademark does not appear in this edition, which has also been called the Ulmer edition (a specimen is in Ulm). It was reprinted in J. Scheible, *Das Kloster* (1846), at which time it was regarded as the oldest Faust book.

W and H sometimes agree verbatim, where Wi diverges. It follows that W and H had a common predecessor X, and that X was not the basis for Wi but could have been at most only a sister stage of that text. In addition, W calls itself an "interpreter" of the Latin text. Between this original Latin version (L) and X, we must therefore postulate a German edition (U), from which Wi, which never cites the Latin Faust-book, must have drawn some material. As a result, it is nearly impossible to distinguish between the expansive translation U and its abbreviated version X, from which W and H were derived. For even though Wi, the classic witness for U, had direct access to H, he substantially revised all his sources (among which are also included records of Faust that circulated under Wagner's name = WF). L tried to condense the Wittenberg stories without (somehow) giving them any local color. U, on the other hand, picked up different localizations. In this effort there was no single governing principle; instead, the material was put together on the basis of loose associations with (and similarities to) the narratives in L.

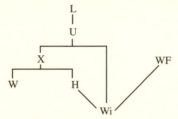

The resemblance of the Faust-book's textual stemma to various Ur-Gospel hypotheses and Two-Source theories may be plainly seen, and since our literary criticism of the Faust-book stands on relatively solid ground, these results have particular methodological weight.

For our further investigations we now set aside the oldest known version of the Faust-book, the Wolfenbüttel manuscript,[30] and start with the one printed in Frankfurt by Spiess in 1587, since it served as the basis for all the subsequent editions of the story. Not counting the three printings already mentioned, this Faust-book was printed a dozen times before Widman's version finally supplanted it in 1599. Questions about its tradition and composition unfortunately cannot always be answered in full, since doubts persist about whether the author found a particular story in the tradition or contrived it himself. He did very little of the latter, as is evident from the ease with which contradictions and doublets can be detected. Chapters 35 and 56, for example, obviously relate the same incident, whether the author found and took up both variants from the tradition or developed the second story himself based on his original impression of the first. The lack of thoroughgoing redaction shows up most of all, however, in the transitions from one story to another, where we can see all the seams in the brickwork.

30. G. Milchsack, ed. (1892–97).

An earlier generation of German scholarship was harshly critical of the book on this point. G. Ellinger[31] speaks of the author's "pitiful style," and W. Scherer[32] calls him a "rank amateur who lacks practically all of the attributes which even an unassuming author needs. How badly he narrates! How poorly he arranges his material!" Erich Schmidt[33] concludes that the loosely strung collection of adventures in Part Three contains "about as much editorial work as bookbinding."

That remark recalls Eduard Schwartz's conclusion about the Gospel of John, or the way in which F. Spitta[34] knocked the Marcan hypothesis on its heels with his shrewd analysis of the Synoptics, particularly his conclusion that the original outline of the story of Jesus is not to be found in the loose arrangement of the Gospel of Mark. Those who advocate an exaggerated version of the Marcan hypothesis find themselves in the very same situation, making a virtue of necessity, as it were, by taking the Marcan outline seriously and forcing themselves to blur over the seams "by means of psychological conjecture."[35] In my opinion, harsh judgments about Mark's defective connections and descriptions have as little place as the equally harsh condemnations of the "amateur" who put together Spiess's Faust-book. In both cases the perspective is all wrong: writers of folk books are not so much authors as they are mere collectors and spokesmen for a tradition that has been carried along by a people. Judgments *in malam partem* are quite pointless and ultimately produce nothing but mistakes.

The ultimate fate of the Spiess Faust-book clearly illustrates my point. Reprints of it were, despite occasional changes or additions, little more than reprints. Then Rudolf Widman[36] intervened more sharply, using handwritten material that was better and more extensive than the writer of the 1587 Faust book had at his command. Two of Widman's extra chapters appeared in the Wolfenbüttel manuscript (which reveals something interesting about the way in which a folk book evolves), but Widman relied primarily on the 1587 edition and tried to improve it in his own ways, getting the chronology right and filling out some stories while omitting others. In 1674 Widman's edition was then worked over in turn by Nikolaus Pfitzer.[37] Around 1725 a brief excerpt from Pfitzer[38] made even more substantial changes: individual stories were arranged by

31. G. Ellinger, *Zeitschrift fur vergleichende Literaturgeschichte u. Renaissance-Literatur* (1887/88), 156.

32. W. Scherer, op. cit., xiiif.

33. E. Schmidt, *Sitzungsberichte der Berliner Akademie der Wissenschaften* (1896), 569.

34. F. Spitta, *Die synoptische Grundschrift* (1912).

35. Albert Schweitzer, *The Quest of the Historical Jesus* (1906), 332.

36. Reprinted in J. Scheible, *Das Kloster* (1846).

37. Newly printed by R. v. Keller, *Bibliothek des literarischen Vereins in Stuttgart* (1880).

38. Published in J. Scheible, *Das Kloster* (1846). A new edition by S. Szamotolski appeared in *Deutsche Literaturdenkmale des 18. u. 19. Jahrh.* 39 (1891).

narrative content, a good deal was left out (there were in fact two long narratives that circulated in Vienna), and the opening sequence was completely rearranged. Modern books and legends about Faust, of which there are many, are generally based on Pfitzer. L. Aurbacher[39] and G. Schwab[40] are just two examples. The title of a work by A. Holder aptly illustrates the manner in which such folk books have to be treated: "The Old Faust-book: Based on Editions from 1587, 1599 and 1674, along with Other Sources from that Era, Revised and Edited in a New (Factual) Arrangement of the Sayings." Thus, we can speak of writing a "harmony" of the Faust books. Finally, it is worth mentioning that some translations of the Faust book into foreign languages (Dutch, English, French) are exact reproductions, whereas others improve on the earlier versions.

These results show that the "synoptic question," which is prompted by the existence of different Faust-books, can now be answered with greater certainty. We have a clear picture of how changes occurred, but explaining why is more difficult. Why this peculiar combination of agreements and divergences? We will have to inquire into the tendencies of individual editions, about which a few things are evident. Since Widman says that Faust studied in Ingolstadt rather than in Wittenberg, obviously this sinful man of the world must have been a Catholic, and Pfitzer's clever calculations prove that the whole story took place in the time "before Luther's blessed Reformation," when the ancient papal system was in full swing. Such views are based on a general impression given by the oldest Faust-book, for it has long been noted that the earliest compiler betrays a decidedly Protestant tendency, and more recent studies have shown that the author of the Wolfenbüttel manuscript is to be sought among the circles of the Gnesio-Lutherans. It may even be correct that the Faust-book is a satire on Melanchthon, using the character of Faust to demonstrate for all to see that Melanchthon's version of the doctrine of justification (free will, synergism, good works as a *conditio sine qua non*) leads to paganism and ultimately to the devil. In any case, it is clear that the whole thing is (indeed, was meant to be) didactic and devotional. Much of the narrative material can be found in Luther's *Tabletalk,* but it is difficult to tell whether *Tabletalk* was a source for the author or merely part of the tradition behind him. Perhaps there were no sources, or possibly we must reckon with a third source common to both.[41] These vexing questions are the same ones that surface in studies of the gospels.

Recognition of the fact that the Faust-book is didactic and instructive has implications for our view of its composition, for like the gospels, this folk book lacks precisely that quality which is essential to a real biography: the effort to tie

39. L. Aurbacher, "Ein Volksbüchlein," *Reclams Universal-Bibliothek* 1291/1292.
40. G. Schwab, "Die Deutschen Volksbücher," *Reclams Universal-Bibliothek* 1515.
41. According to G. Kawerau in his debate with Milchsack's book (*Theol. Literatur-Zeitung* [1897]: cols. 488ff.), it is firmly established that the author of the Faust-book "had read and fully exploited" Aurifaber's collection of Luther's *Tabletalk.*

together (both internally and externally) individual stories from the life of the hero. Faligan, the French Faust scholar whom I have already cited twice, has aptly described the situation: "There is no chronological order . . . yet the book is not bereft of all compositional merit. The author . . . follows a very clear plan, but it is a plan for religious and moral edification, so the author is more attentive to the private life of the hero than to his public persona."[42] This form of composition is essentially based on the tradition, which was made up of an assortment of small units.

A synopsis of the various Faust-books makes clear that their publishers were "authors" only in the very slightest sense; basically they were collectors, tradents, and redactors. The traditional units that they brought together already had attained a formal consistency, but the framework into which the individual units were set was diverse and indeterminate. To verify this point, I constructed my own synopsis of eight different Faust-books: (1) Spiess 1587; (2) the new Ulm edition 1587; (3) Widman 1599; (4) Pfitzer 1674; (5) "Christian-Meynenden" 1725; (6) Aurbacher 1825; (7) G. Schwab 1835/37; and (8) Holder 1907. It has already been mentioned that the Ulm edition arranges the stories differently than Spiess's original printing. However—and this proves that the framework is indeterminate—the rearrangement of the stories does not change their introductions, including details of time or place; the pieces travel, as it were, with their own framework.[43] Everywhere we look, we see that the situational details can be either precise or vague. Very often there is no mention of time at all; but then another story suddenly provides us with the month, day, and year. If we follow one story down through the various editions, we often find that a later Faust-book leaves out specifications of time given by an earlier one; yet details of time often show up for the first time in later editions, either to stick fast or drop out again later. The same goes for descriptions of places and people. We notice, therefore, a two-way process at work: specific situational details become attached to some stories that previously did not have them, but they also disappear from stories that previously were outfitted with them.

It is exactly the same with the gospels. Thus we learn from the Faust-books that an excess or surfeit of framing details cannot be the basis for firm conclusions about either the temporal setting of a story or the historical worth of a tradition. The vexed question of whether Mark or Matthew is more original (either because Mark has such a wealth of situational details or because Matthew has so few) can never be settled, since the course of the tradition shows equal tendencies toward expansion and abbreviation. This kind of evidence also cannot solve the problem of priority, since general specifications of time ("on one occasion" is especially frequent) serve only as caesuras, whether they appear as introductions or conclusions to pericopes. None of this was changed when the reports were collected, not even in the later editions. As far as order was concerned, it

42. Faligan, *Histoire de la légende de Faust* (1888), 151.
43. Cf., in this regard, the cases collected in my *Der Rahmen der Geschichte Jesu*.

took the form of an arrangement by content—Matthew even more than Mark arranged the material by subject, rejecting various unnecessary framing pieces, and became (with good reason) the favorite evangelist of the Christian church.

Richard Benz, the last editor of the Faust-book, had the right sense of the matter when (unlike the Germanists I have already mentioned, Ellinger, Scherer, and Erich Schmidt) he did not waste time criticizing the outline of the first printing but instead laid down the unabbreviated outline of his own "restoration," making use of later printings when they offered new material: "Since oral tradition is the common element, the unity of the poem remains secure, even though it was obviously created out of different sources: the individual adventures are linked in a connection which sprang from the organization of the work. Thus the reader has in hand the folk book of Dr. Faust in its original stylistic form and in its fullest material completeness."[44]

44. R. Benz, *Die Deutschen Volksbücher* (1912).

8

LEGENDS OF THE SAINTS.

With regard to origin and literary character, popular Christian hagiography from antiquity and the Middle Ages is no different from the folk book of Doctor Faust. Here again we are dealing with oft-read and continually expanding devotional literature of the people. We have already discussed the boundary between hagiography and literary biographies of saints, and we have quoted the opinions of scholars who hold that a comparison between the gospels and popular lives of saints can be productive. At this point we can now delineate their literary properties and illustrate them with some typical examples.

The *Acta sanctorum* of the Bollandists are some of the best examples of collected hagiography, but in that work of applied Jesuit scholarship it is not always easy to pick out the folk traditions and collected traditions because the *Acta* of individual saints are arranged for the calendar year and are diligently and seriously presented as unbroken praise. For our purposes, "The Holy Life and Sufferings otherwise known as The Passion" and especially the famous *Legenda aurea* of *Jacobus a Voragine*[45] are more suitable. We owe these learned and concise works of hagiography to the Bollandist H. Delehaye,[46] who assessed the content and development of "hagiographic legends" and the redactional work of the hagiographer with a methodological precision that has much to teach scholars of the gospels. Indeed, it is regrettable that this discerning Catholic scholar was denied the chance to see his critical work freely applied to the gospels.

In order to understand hagiography, it is essential to understand its religious character and its devotional purpose, since hagiographies are monuments that on the one hand were inspired by the cult of the saints, and on the other hand also served to promote that cult. As with the gospels, we can see that it was the people who originally created and bore along the tradition, and only later did they become hagiographers or biographers of saints or recorders of legends. As the anonymous author, the people were a secretive collecting agent—fashioning, transforming and expanding the material; yet it was not always possible to

45. Unfortunately, the Latin version of Th. Grässe (3rd ed., 1890) is out of print, but Richard Benz produced two distinguished volumes in translation (Jena: Diederichs, 1912).

46. H. Delehaye, *Les légendes hagiographiques* (1905; 2nd ed., 1906), was translated into German by E. A. Stückelberg under the title, *Die hagiographischen Legenden* (1907).

capture in writing exactly what had been created. Sometimes the hagiographer, who comes upon the *membra disiecta* and seeks to fit them into a unified whole, has to do nothing more than collect and compose what has been handed down. In this way both the popular mind and scholarly effort have an impact on hagiographies.

In the very beginning, when the legends are just beginning to develop, an unconscious and unreflective process affects the narrative by introducing a subjective element into the objective facts. The result is a method of description that is neither totally false nor completely in agreement with reality: each person, each community, relates its own legend. In everyday life we see examples of this kind of unconscious influence all the time. As the number of middlemen increases, so does the potential for error, as each one tells the story in his own way. Indifference or just plain poor memory can cause details to be lost so that subsequent narrators, trying to correct mistakes that they notice but cannot always fully comprehend, introduce or invent new details. This everyday occurrence becomes momentous if it takes place in significant numbers and if the relatively uninhibited impressions of the people take the place of the rather restrained mental activity of an individual author. Imagination can gain ground, an observation that is particularly apropos of the gospels.[47]

For all its freedom, however, imagination (like a child) does have its limits, as we can see from its impact on legends. The number of characters that appear is not unlimited. In popular memory, heroes replace each other; they do not stand side by side. We notice a tendency toward simplification. Chronological and geographical considerations are minimal. The popular mind sets historical materials

---

47. It is significant that even so conservative a scholar as A. Schlatter (*Die Theologie des Neuen Testaments, II. Teil* [1910], 532) understands this fact: "None of the Evangelists was afraid of the possibility that imagination might have been involved in their depictions of Jesus. Instead they actively promoted it for themselves and for their readers, not only because no one could relate these stories in sober truthfulness without any imagination, but also because both the narrator and the readers were actively interested in these stories, and the impact of that interest always resulted in a somewhat showy picture. . . . In many cases we should stop trying to fine-tune the boundary where memory turns into fiction and the constructed shape of the narrative parts company with the actual course of events." Schlatter says that this imagination was "subject to a rigorous discipline" and that it was rooted in the fabric of the description of Christ for believers, and he contends that the distinction between myth and reality would never have been forgotten, but his biblicist stance is too vague for me to commit myself to it. In addition, Schlatter consciously applies his statements about imagination and faith only to the gospel writers themselves, not to the earlier material that was handed down anonymously. He says: "There can be no hypothesis, however necessary, about a freely reigning legend (on the analogy of the Midrash); such ideas must be abandoned to the empty space which lies behind the known history of the Gospels." I assert that that "empty space" gives the impression of emptiness only because it is so dark. We have to let ourselves float in it; when we do, our field of vision is transformed.

next to each other and weaves them into a loose fabric. The connections between them are blurry and inessential, so that the picture stands out all the more strongly.[48] Designations of place may appear, but it must not be forgotten that even when they are quite specific, such localizations are usually of literary origin.[49] On the other hand, popular memory can be remarkably tenacious in hanging on to them. A hagiographer, like a writer of legends, belongs in the domain of the popular, except that he has authorial aspirations and even some success. The extent of that success is the decisive point, and it is precisely here that Luke parts company with Mark and Matthew. Yet even Luke could not efface the character of the preliminary stages.

48. Cf., in this regard, the consistent picture in the gospel pericopes.

49. See Delahaye, *Les légendes hagiographiques,* 51: "Is it still necessary to keep on making plain just how illusory is the process of tracing the itinerary of a saint by means of legendary signposts? Sometimes the attempt is still made, but not exactly for historical purposes." It is worth remarking that Delahaye knows that the life of St. Radegunde might become the object of such misguided efforts (cf. *Analecta Boll. B.X.,* 56–60). This is strongly reminiscent of the questions dealt with in *Der Rahmen der Geschichte Jesu.*

9

ANCIENT CHRISTIAN MONASTIC STORIES:
HISTORIA MONACHORUM and *HISTORIA LAUSIACA;*
APOPHTHEGMATA PATRUM.

Early Christian monastic histories, which are (strictly speaking) precursors to the lives of the saints, have these same characteristics, a fact that is plainly evident in recent treatments of Rufinus's *Historia Monachorum* and Palladius's *Historia Lausiaca* by E. Preuschen,[50] R. Reitzenstein,[51] and W. Bousset.[52] It is noteworthy that current research increasingly emphasizes the anonymous preliminary stages of these documents rather than their authors, a clear indication that scholars have come to understand the difference between tradition and composition, the passage from low literature to high literature:

> No particular individual or original collection stands at the origin of these documents. Beginning with separate short stories, a form of folk literature developed which was then gathered by different collectors into corpora of various sizes as it made the transition into actual literature. The fact that we know one of these collectors by name (Rufinus) is important enough, but we should not overestimate his influence. He can be credited with no more than tying together various sources into the framework of a narrative, and perhaps adding an admonition or devotional thought here and there, before finally unifying the basic conception and outlook. . . . Exactly the same goes for the author of the *Historia Lausiaca.*[53]

Thus Rufinus was a "well-educated author with an interest in philosophy"[54] who was certainly capable of producing something more original and consistent.

Our impression of Luke's literary skills comes to mind here. His considerable capabilities are only slightly evident in his gospel and Acts (certainly more

50. E. Preuschen, *Palladius und Rufinus* (1897).
51. R. Reitzenstein, *Hellenistische Wundererzählungen* (1906), 74–80. Reitzenstein, *Historia Monachorum und Historia Lausiaca* (1916).
52. W. Bousset, "Komposition und Charakter der *Historia Lausiaca.*" *Nachr. von der Gesellsch. der Wissenschaften zu Göttingen* (1917), 173–217; Bousset, "Zur Komposition der *Historia Lausiaca,*" ZNW 23 (1922): 81–98.
53. Reitzenstein, *Historia Monachorum*, 76f.
54. Ibid., 78.

strongly in the latter) because he was, on the whole, essentially just a tradent of the tradition that had been passed down to him. It may also be noted that the first words of the *Historia Lausiaca* (Πολλῶν πολλὰ καί ποικίλα κατὰ διαφόρους καιρούς συγγράμματα καταλελοιπότων) recall the opening sentence of the Gospel of Luke. In both cases the pen of the author plainly gives itself away, particularly in longer reflective passages where we often meet the author's "I." In many places the author introduces personal recollections—real or alleged—into preexisting traditions, so that the narrative looks like a thoroughly personal report. In reality, of course, these personal tidbits were not all written by the author himself.

Closely related in both form and content to the *Historia Lausiaca* is the so-called *Apophthegmata Patrum,* a collection of sayings and deeds that stands as a monument to ascetic monasticism. This tradition originated in monastic circles and was handed down orally for quite some time. Since most monks were uneducated fellahin who did not speak Greek very well and who left nothing behind in writing, these *apophthegmata,* coming as they do from a nonliterary stratum, are a good example of the origin and development of an oral tradition. The earliest beginnings of the collection reach back into the last third of the fourth century. At the other end of the development stands the μέγα λειμωνάριον, the "Paradise of the Father" at the turn of the fifth and sixth centuries.

During this period the form of the work gave rise to many new editions, and an extensive tradition made up of 1,500 to 2,000 anecdotes and sayings was published in several versions and collections by a host of witnesses. Individual redactors did not, however, draw directly from the oral tradition. Often they first had to do the laborious work of collecting documents. Small collections had already become fixed in writing by the end of the fourth century, even though the living oral tradition continued to thrive for some time thereafter. Everything was in a continual state of flux: new pieces kept coming into view, surfacing here and there, and each witness had its own special material. The collection had not yet become literary in the strict sense, and the collectors were every bit as nonliterary as the tradition they received. In this respect they were completely different from Rufinus or Palladius, who allowed various kinds of subjective factors to affect their efforts.

In the *Apophthegmata Patrum* we have the material in its earliest imprint. They resemble, not the finished gospels, but rather their preliminary stages. Like the gospels, the *Apophthegmata* also have an unusually complicated textual history. In both cases we are dealing with books that were meant to be read aloud. Medieval monks loved to read the *Apophthegmata Patrum* aloud in their cloisters, and this kind of usage had the consequence of causing the work, which by its very nature always tended to produce new versions, to vary even more.

The only way to get the right perspective on the form of a collection like this is to study (as Bousset has done) its textual history. By the time later editions began to appear in languages different from that of the original, the textual tradition had become like that of the German folk book Doktor Faust or, more significantly, as complex as that of the gospels. Detailed studies of traditions like these absolutely must attend to the textual question.[55] But the main point is still clear: over and over again we find that the foundation is made up of small units, short individual anecdotes and single sayings, which are only loosely framed. It could not have been the other way around, as some would like to suggest: the μέγα λειμωνάριον cannot be a collection of real βίοι from which the apophthegms were extracted.[56] As everyone knows, questions like these also have to be answered in gospel studies.

55. R. Knopf is right to point out that we "do not possess a text of the Gospels which is adequate for highly detailed studies." Cf. R. Knopf, *Einführung in das Neue Testament* 2nd ed., ed. H. Weinel and H. Lietzmann (1923), 111.

56. I have already mentioned Bousset's essay, "Die Textüberlieferung der *Apophthegmata Patrum*," in which he refutes the attempt to move in this direction. His short essay gives a good idea of how such an effort leads into "an almost shoreless sea." On the basis of extensive catalogues and tables, Bousset offers a solution to the principal problem, "but there lies before me a laborious project, which may or may not be publishable at the present time."

Lately, however, a printing of this laborious project has very fortunately been obtained. Through the kindness of Gustav Krüger, it was possible for me, after I finished the present work, to see the first page proofs. The first book is entitled, "Studien zur Geschichte des ältesten Mönchtums" and offers "Untersuchungen über Textüberlieferung und Charakter der *Apophthegmata Patrum*." The question of the gospels is treated on page 77: "A comparison with our Synoptic Gospels can certainly clarify this (i.e., the character of the *Apophthegmata Patrum* as the raw material of an oral tradition). In general we are convinced that the Synoptic Gospels are the rather direct precipitate of an oral tradition. But how well formed was this tradition? Even the Gospel of Mark can rightly be called an artistic vita, and even though the teachings of Jesus were certainly conglomerated out of individual sayings, for the most part we have speeches and not the individual sayings. A rather extensive literary process thus lies between the original tradition and our gospels. In the *Apophthegmata*, however, the raw material of an oral tradition is much more directly accessible. We have to dig for the ground floor of our Gospel tradition—the individual anecdote, the individual saying, the individual short dialogue, the individual parable—but in the *Apophthegmata* it all steps directly forward in tangible reality. Hundreds upon hundreds of fragments of the oral tradition stand disconnected from each other, all mixed up in completely arbitrary order. Later they were gradually gathered by content into groups of various sizes, but the individual short units almost always remain undisturbed."

Bousset then pursued a style-critical analysis of the individual pieces of the tradition and concluded: "On every page our observations have repeatedly demonstrated the utterly unique value of the *Apophthegmata* tradition. In it we actually have the direct precipitate of an oral tradition over a wide range, including in the vast majority of cases individual sayings (pneumatic speech), individual short conversations, brief dialogues, individual parables, individual character anecdotes, and short miracle stories. All of these were protected through memory in the tradition. Elaborate legends, speeches, sermons, and polished literary reports of visions are almost entirely absent, or take up barely any room." In the light of recent achievements in form-critical studies of the gospels, the essential similarity between the two complexes of tradition is recognizable.

This similarity ultimately relates to the purely oral sources of the gospel tradition. Bousset has very carefully demonstrated that the earliest linguistic dress of the *Apophthegmata Patrum* was Coptic and that Greeks were the first to pick up the earliest larger written collections of this oral tradition. "Once again the comparison with our Synoptic Gospels suggests itself. They originate with Aramaic oral tradition, but the documents as we now have them are in Greek. The Gospel of Mark is and always will be a Greek Gospel: an Aramaic "Ur-Mark" is a dream and a fantasy. Only a Greek, or perhaps a Jew imbued with Greek culture, would have had the formal talent and creative power to write a life of Jesus. Even the sayings as we know them, as they appear in Matthew and Luke, are a Greek document and not merely a translation. With our tools we can go no further . . . It is always the same phenomenon: Greeks created literature which the simple oriental circles in which the tradition arose were in no position to create. And so also in individual cases did Greeks put the final stamp on this literature. The transition of this tradition from one language into another was not merely an act of translation, but rather an act of freely treating and transmitting previously fluid material. One may suppose that from the beginning translational errors were very rare (in my opinion this has been proved by a detailed examination of the Synoptics. Most putative errors of translation are questionable. I suppose that the same result would be obtained in the *Apophthegmata*). But this stamp freely touched only the surface; beneath it there remained the character of the original oral tradition in another language. We are dealing here with an extremely simple tradition, with unpretentious narratives and simple short sayings. This tradition did not lose much of its own character, even when it was translated into another language. But again, in neither case do we have anything from the original tradition in its original language" (p. 90f). I think Bousset's observations hit the nail directly on the head and are quite productive. I would put a question mark after the statement that only a Greek or a Hellenized Jew could have mustered up that "formal talent" which Bousset himself once rightly described—when referring to both the gospels and the *Apophthegmata*—as nothing special. Certainly Bousset has accurately described the gospels and the *Apophthegmata Patrum,* and it has to be granted that "simple oriental circles" could not have carried to completion these compositional accomplishments. But there were other oriental circles to which that generalization does not apply. Recall, for example, the circles that created the collected stories of the 1001 Nights.

In conclusion, one must appreciate the great strength and tender care with which Bousset has carried out his whole painstaking investigation. It is very important to him to appreciate the *apophthegmata* tradition, a "source which has been unduly neglected until now." "Put Athanasius' *Life of Antony,* a work of art in which historical reality is completely lost, the travel novellas of Rufinus and Palladius and many others on one side of the scale, and the *Apophthegmata Patrum* on the other, and I am confident that the *Apophthegmata* will sink and the others will rise very rapidly. . . . Out of all these sources [Bousset had previously also mentioned the *Life of Pachomius,* which he esteems very highly as well], I give the *Apophthegmata Patrum* the crown and palm. None of them can measure up to the bulk, breadth, diversity, and fidelity of its material" (91f.). In my judgment, it is clear that only a historian of religion could carry out this kind of form-critical work. For the answers have to do, not with "formal" (i.e., external) questions, but with historical-religious and theological ones. This justifies my remarks below about the value of the gospel tradition: it is not a matter of theological indifference that Luke introduced the "world" into the gospel record.

10

The Franciscan legends.

Most scholars who study medieval lives of saints do so because of their content, which is important in its own right. But these documents also pose questions of the sort we have been discussing. Despite countless studies, however, the issues have not yet been fully resolved or even convincingly laid out. How many times has the Francis tradition been compared to the Jesus tradition! The two figures almost seem to compel the comparison, and as early as the end of the fourteenth century, the book *Conformitates* made such a comparison its explicit goal. From then on it gradually came to be recognized that we are dealing here with two traditions of the same form. Indeed, comparing them is remarkably instructive precisely because they have both developed to such an extent that Francis studies[57] and Jesus research now have a great deal in common. Take the difficulty of research, for example: literary problems in the Francis tradition are not any simpler than those in the Jesus tradition. The narratives about the saint from Assisi pose a "synoptic problem" because they contain broad stretches of parallel and interdependent material that seem to defy even the most refined methods.

The Francis tradition has been more thoroughly examined than any other in medieval source criticism, and the methods, goals, and results of this research broadly correspond to those of gospels research. The accomplishments to this point seem vastly complex, perhaps even to the point of chaos. Toward the close of the nineteenth century, for example, new discoveries, studies, and hypotheses were appearing almost every year. Theories were overthrown and reconstructed in rapid succession, and (just as in gospel studies) there was some feeling that research was simply going in a circle, a *circulus vitiosus,* and this turn of events gave rise to skepticism. Different scholars preferred different "sources," but the two biographies by Thomas of Celano and the biography by Bonaventure were universally well regarded. By contrast, nowadays it is the *Legenda trium sociorum* and the *Speculum perfectionis* that are hotly disputed. Recently, in fact, the relationship between these two documents and the biographies of Celano and Bonaventure has been clarified, and the results cast a questioning light on ideas that were once thought to be secure.

57. In what follows, cf. Walter Goetz, *Die Quellen zur Geschichte des hl. Franz von Assisi* (1904). Goetz is a Protestant historian, but his book has been read with interest by Catholics as well.

Where is a firm standard of judgment to be found? One side regards the oldest witness, i.e., the *Vita prima* of Celano, as the most reliable; while the other, under the influence of church tradition, prefers Bonaventure. The *Vita secunda* has been criticized on the basis of scientific insights and the principle "older is better," but the *Prima* has also been attacked, and high value has been placed on (of all things) the later compilations. Thus, every scholar has picked out a personal favorite. Paul Sabatier argues tirelessly for the *Speculum perfectionis,* just as F. Spitta does for the Gospel of Luke. There is, of course, an "official" ecclesiastical opinion in favor of Bonaventure (because his biography was most widely used in the first century after Francis), just as the Gospel of Matthew early on became the favorite gospel of the church. But Protestant as well as Catholic scholarship has shattered that position: a legend that was generally regarded as worthless because it first appeared during the fourteenth century (the *Speculum perfectionis*) suddenly received a promotion (courtesy of Sabatier) and was placed in the year 1227, while the relatively old *Legenda trium sociorum* was reduced to the ranks by the Catholic scholar, van Ortroy. The traditions preserved by Thomas of Celano were attacked so freely that at times things veered into extreme skepticism, as for example, when the Italian scholar Tamassia branded our earliest source an impudent plagiarist who constructed his account from various documents in obedience to the pope's order that saints be canonized in literature.

While all these hypotheses were quite bold and pointed, other scholars have argued for caution and compromise. Dogmatic, ethical, and particularly scientific questions all come into play here, and naturally Catholic and Protestant scholars have gone their separate ways. Did the Franciscan movement begin with active labor or mendicant poverty? To answer that question, one has to evaluate sources, just as scholars of early Christianity have to assess various traditions when studying the Ebionites. Protestants, doubtful of the miracle stories in the *Vita prima,* seek out a saint who is untainted by such things; whereas Catholics regard these very miracle stories as the most original. Just as in gospels research, preconceived ideas tend to cloud over the study of sources, and even scholars directly involved in the research can be unsure about how to distinguish between sources (e.g., does a change in the narrator's perspective signify a change in the source?).

Interested observers have more than enough reason to be skeptical. What are they supposed to think, when scholars can speak of a "*parfum franciscain*" and treat it as authoritative evidence? Expressions like that are reminiscent of gospels scholars who, after a brainstorm or two, confidently declare that some gospel story is "incomprehensible." There is, however, no reason to despair of an answer to the literary question. Ultimately all serious (if imperfect) literary studies do have their good points. Tamassia's thesis about the inferiority of Celano has been generally rejected, but it still compels us to study the literary construction of the medieval legend. In a similar way, unsuccessful theories about Ur-Mark or Ur-Luke (cf. Spitta) still make a contribution to scholarship.

Furthermore, it must also be pointed out that the undergrowth of Francis scholarship is not impenetrable: there are pathways and clearings, and definite conclusions have been reached, particularly about the sources. Compare, for example, the books by H. Tilemann,[58] a Protestant, and F. van den Borne,[59] a Catholic. Van den Borne depends on Tilemann in important respects, and there is no mistaking the extensive range of agreement between them. It is no different with work on the gospels. The Markan hypothesis is actually not a hypothesis anymore if it can be adopted (however bashfully) by Catholic scholars.

But it is more significant that even with all this scholarship, the literary critical questions have not yet been fully settled. In addition to the question of sources, there are also questions of style criticism and form criticism that scholars of the Francis tradition have only begun to answer. Not all scholars have become attentive to the living milieu of the Franciscan legend out of which the strings of sayings and series of stories have been formed. Some still refer to "sources for the story of St. Francis" without recognizing these "sources" for what they actually are: expressions of Franciscan piety. Gospels research is a little further ahead on this point, as recent form-critical work shows. Certainly the most important question is the one about the character of Jesus and of Francis. To that end, however, we must eavesdrop on the "sources," and the sound of their voice will be lost if we do not strain to hear the tradition itself, for its own sake.

When studying the Francis tradition (or the gospels, or the folk books, or the monastic stories, or the lives of the saints), the first order of business is always the question of tradition and composition. Each author's stated purposes have to be examined closely. Thomas of Celano, for example, begins the *Vita prima* as follows:

> Since no one could ever possibly remember everything that he said and did, it was my desire to write an orderly, pious, and completely true account of the deeds and life of our blessed father Francis, or at least of those things which I myself had heard from his own mouth or from reliable and trusted witnesses. And so by the order of the Lord and glorious Pope Gregory, I have endeavored to record as much as I could, or as much as my imperfect words would allow. Would that I might deserve to be the disciple of one who spoke so plain and true and had nothing to do with fancy words! Everything which I was able to find out about that blessed man is all laid out here in three little books, each arranged in chapters, so that the variety of times, topics, and deeds will not make for confusion and the truth will not be lost in obscurity.[60]

58. H. Tilemann, *Studien zur Individualität des Franziskus von Assisi* (1914).

59. F. van den Borne, *Die Franziskus-Forschung in ihrer Entwicklung dargestellt* (1917).

60. Cf. *Acta Sanctorum* II, Octave, 683f. New edition: *S. Francisci Assisiensis Vita et Miracula . . . auctore Fr. Thoma de Celano edidit Ed. Alenconiensis* (Rome, 1906).

He then goes on to say that the first book contains a series of stories (*historiae ordo*), along with some of the many miracles done by Francis. The second book is also largely chronological. The third book, he explains, relates many of the miracles (and could have related many more) that Francis performed after he had gone to heaven to reign with Christ. All of this ends with the confession that the *Vita* has been written for the adoration, glory, and honor of Francis.

Like Luke, Thomas of Celano takes care to state that he intends to write a *vita seriatim* (cf. Luke 1:3: καθεξῆς); he cites witnesses and acknowledges that his account is incomplete. In sum, his introduction is a mixture of authorial consciousness and cautious respect for the material. He frankly admits that the material is arranged more by content than by temporal sequence. Indeed, temporal connections do not appear even where we would expect to find them. Apart from a very general time sequence that could hardly have been avoided, the goal of *seriatim* is never attained. Instead, catchword introductions like "one time" and "one day" are typical, and the most typical feature of all is the fact that sometimes the individual pictures are framed, and sometimes they are not. The individual story is the essence, and—just like the gospels—the framework is not essential but secondary and indefinite. It is no different with the *Vita secunda:* the story moves from one scene to the next without regard to temporal sequence, and the introduction leaves no room for doubt about what is coming.

The *Legenda trium sociorum,* which was written during the period between Celano's two biographies, also appears to be a compilation. It draws on witnesses from an older generation and blurs the individual characteristics of the three companions: Leo, Rufinus, and Angelus. It matters little whether this document corrected earlier works or simply ignored them, since it states even more strongly than Celano that it has not recorded (and never intended to record) a chronological sequence of events: "Rather than following a continuous narrative, we have instead picked as it were from a pleasant meadow only the flowers which we thought were the most lovely."[61] It is worth remembering here that full blossoms grow out of little flowers. In the *Legenda triorum sociorum* the material has undergone substantial changes, omissions, and expansions, but it is not convincing to assert that a tradition formed in this way lacks historical value.[62]

The final redaction of the account presents the legend of Bonaventure, and there is essentially no new material. Instead, the author simply works at harmonizing the existing witnesses, and even his finished and published work can (and must) be described as a mosaic. Among the later editions, which are fed not only by written but also by oral traditions, the most important is the hotly disputed *Speculum perfectionis.* An assessment of this document, particularly with respect to chronology, would conclude that in all probability a large part of it is old and valuable.

61. Cf. *Acta Sanctorum* II, Octave, 723.
62. *Contra* W. Goetz, *Die Quellen zur Geschichte des hl. Franz von Assisi,* 96.

In view of this situation, what are we to say about the author? It is indeed curious that Thomas of Celano, who clearly had some ability as a writer, did not arrange his two biographies in better chronological and psychological order. And what about Bonaventure? W. Goetz says of him: "Bonaventure has long been famous for taking on the work of writing up the Francis legend, and the way in which he sought to accomplish this mission is an interesting literary-historical problem in its own right. But it is precisely at this point that our hopes are utterly dashed. True, his version does display a preference for fine style, the kind of rhetoric which was required at that time, and a very good arrangement and distribution of the material; but the content which fills out this nice form is really nothing but a compilation which falls quite short of today's standards."[63] After serving up a few more remarks of praise and blame, Goetz asserts: "Bonaventure could have surpassed his contemporaries if he had constructed the chronology of his narrative more tightly, but instead his use of time and sequence is every bit as vague as that of his predecessors."

As necessary as it is to critically evaluate the individual pieces, casting aspersions in this way is, it seems to me, totally out of place. As we have seen, it is pointless to grumble about the first publisher of the Faust-book, or for that matter about the individual evangelists, playing one against the other, preferring first Mark over Luke and then Luke over Mark, just because the chronology and psychology of one seems a little better than the other. There are two considerations that force us to start from a different point: (1) All of these "authors" would have had intentions exactly the opposite of these proposals if their objective, generally speaking, was edification. And still more important, (2) these "authors" had no choice but to restrain themselves (indeed, they more or less *wanted* to restrain themselves), because they were carried along by a tradition that had been formed a long time before, a tradition they could not even think about altering in any substantial way.

63. Goetz, *Die Quellen zur Geschichte,* 245f.

11

GOETHE AND THE LEGENDS OF ST. ROCHUS; MARTIN BUBER AND THE HASIDIC LEGENDS OF THE GREAT MAGGID.

I would like to illustrate this last remark with an authorial personality like Goethe, who on one occasion found himself under the influence of this law of self-restraint in the face of the material. We can be grateful to Goethe for his report on the "St. Rochus Festival in Bingen,"[64] a legendary narrative that makes for an entertaining and instructive example of restraint in the use of tradition. Goethe sits down with participants in the festival and asks for information about the saint:

> The whole community was more than happy to recount the legend; indeed, it became something of a competition as parents and children all joined in. Here we meet the real essence of a saga as it moves from mouth to mouth and ear to ear. Contradictions did not come up, but endless variations did, which may be due to the fact that each person told a different part of the story or a different episode, and one emphasized this detail and another one that, so that even the travels of the saint (where he went, and when) were all mixed up. I could not possibly succeed in relating the story as I heard it, i.e., as a recorded conversation; it could only be told in the form in which it was customarily handed down, and that is the form in which it stands written here.

As far as internal and external sequences of events are concerned, the tradition Goethe is describing has characteristics that are by now familiar to us. Note in particular that the itinerary is not thoroughly consistent. A couple of well-known places are mentioned, but the location of some events is not stated. Local color, however, is not entirely lacking. Goethe is cautious and insightful in criticizing his own work, as is shown by his remarks about the festival sermon: "We believed that we had grasped his [the preacher's] meaning, and sometimes we repeated his words among friends. But it is possible that during such transmissions, we may have departed from his original text and woven in something of our own."

---

64. *Goethe's Works* (Sophia Edition), Part I, 34, 1, p. 1ff. I am grateful to A. Deissmann for pointing out this "analogy" to me.

I would like to conclude my discussion of analogies to the gospels with Martin Buber's book on the great Maggid,[65] which makes clear just how dubious it is to think that the writer of a folk book or legend has to try to organize his book according to our idea of a periodizing, portraitizing, and psychologizing biography. The Maggid was a particularly important figure in the Hasidic movement, and Buber opens his book with a stimulating preface that shines a bright light directly on our problem:

> For the most part the legend originates in a period when the formation of a literary style of narration was either already virtually complete or at least decisively shaped. In the first case, the legend would have been only slightly impacted by the narrative style; but in the second place it would have been quite overcome by it. Buddhist legends, Indian fables, Franciscan legends, and early Italian novellas may all belong together, but the Hasidic legend is something completely different. In this period Diaspora Judaism had only begun to develop a literary style of narration with roots in the realm of the popular. What the Hasidim had to say in praise of their masters (the Zaddikim) could not be limited to any form; as legend it could not shape itself into something else, the way folk poetry did. It remained raw ore, and noble ore it is, as it has come into my possession in a couple of hundred folk books and personal communications. The authors of the folk books were no more highly esteemed than itinerant singers. Most of them hauled from town to town and hawked their wares, which the people treated as trivial goods, unlike the sacred writings of the Hasidic teachers. (Of course almost all of the books of Hasidic legends were published in Hebrew; most of the Yiddish translations were highly condensed and watered down). Only one or two of the very oldest translations were treated with any respect; at most they were "believed in." The later ones sought to make themselves more credible by citing the words of an original narrator or, where possible, an eyewitness. (Some modern collections, whose systematic construction requires something a little more scientific, consist of groups of them). The oral tradition is quite different. Here authenticity is personally attested, as each narrator speaks of "his" rabbi and the narrative has the aura of holy story. The "seer" of Lublin supposedly once saw a brightness shining out of a cell;[66] when he entered, he saw Hasidim in there telling stories about their Zaddikim.[67]

I know of no quotation that illustrates better than these compelling remarks by Buber how folk books come down to us, borne along by a community. In fact, they are not well-formed material but raw ore, served up in oral tradition, in personal communications, in folk books; completely ignored (and thereby quite valuable); thoroughly shaped in this case by the cult; made polymorphous by the

---

65. M. Buber, *Der grosse Maggid und seine Nachfolge* (1922), vi–ix.
66. "Cell," i.e., a prayer closet for a cloistered community of prayer.
67. Buber, *Der grosse Maggid,* vi–viii.

involvement of more than one early narrator; and yet, on the whole, quite unmistakable. The author, who knows what is most important and what is less so, submits to the original tradition:

> I have learned to consider it my purpose—indeed it is incumbent upon me—to
> give appropriate form (nothing more, nothing less) to the stories which I select
> from the vast wealth of material. I do not "compose," and I do not add anything
> to the motifs already there; I merely fuse them into the form of a narrative. In
> the Maggid tradition it is a matter of "legendary novellas" and (more predomi-
> nantly) of "legendary anecdotes." And it is utterly essential to realize that both
> of these are highly condensed genres, i.e., narratives in outline. Not only does
> this form dispense with everything psychological, but everything ornamental as
> well.[68]

It does not need to be pointed out how strongly these remarks apply to the gospel tradition. In this situation, the life of the one whom the legend concerns cannot possibly be described as a biography, but it is still important to put together the "image of a life": "Sometimes the material seemed to construct itself out of selected stories into a life which could almost perfectly be described as the pure development of a soul . . . or else as task and fulfillment . . . ; other times gaps remained."[69] In that comment one can trace both the extent and the limits of the task of the folk book researcher and narrator, the legend researcher and writer, the gospel researcher and the writer of a life of Jesus.

68. Ibid., viii.
69. Ibid., ix.

12

THE CULTIC CHARACTER OF LEGENDS OF SAINTS, *APOPHTHEGMATA PATRUM,* AND THE GOSPELS.

Goethe's report about the way the St. Rochus legend was recounted by pilgrims, along with what Buber had to say about the growth and development of the Hasidic Maggid legend, leads us a bit further, to the cultic character of these traditions. It raises the question of whether this might not be the place where a notable analogy to the gospels is to be found. So far as these matters have received any attention recently, the tendency has been to disassociate the gospels from *chreiai,* folk books, and stories of saints and monks, mainly because of the gospels' cultic and mythic content. Bultmann's conclusion that the gospels are cult-legends has been productive and influential: "Mark created this genre; the Christ-myth gave his book, the book of secret epiphanies, a unity which is not truly biographical but which is grounded in myth."[70] In light of this fact, scholars have largely abandoned attempts to find analogies in Greek memoirs, Hellenistic biographies, and even in *chreiai* like the life of Aesop, not to mention oriental folk books (cf. the Ahikar novel). Indeed, as the first part of our investigation thoroughly demonstrated, most of these suggested parallels are not really possible. To be sure, we had thought that the Ahikar novel (with certain limitations) and the *chreiai* (which, as Bultmann thought, have "neither a biographical interest nor the technique to carry it out") had to be considered as analogies.

Myth and cult are certainly not the essential element as far as these documents are concerned, yet it can still be shown that they are valuable analogies. But first we must ask: Is there not cultic content in all the lives of saints we have mentioned? Bultmann appears to answer this question in the negative when he asserts: "It appears to me that we need analogies in order to understand the individual pieces of the Gospel tradition, but not the gospels as wholes. The gospels as wholes grew out of the immanent urge toward development which inhered in the tradition, and out of the Christ-cult and Christ-myth of Hellenistic Christianity. They are thus an original creation of Christianity."[71] The question of whether we need analogies can be disputed. If they can be denied for the gospels as wholes, the same can be said for the individual pieces of the synoptic tradition.

---

70. Bultmann, *Die Geschichte der synoptischen Tradition* (1921), 227.
71. Ibid., 373–74.

Furthermore, the judgment that they are "an original creation of Christianity" in no way entails that there are no analogies to that creation. It only means that genealogical methods cannot be applied to this original creation and that it cannot be represented as dependent upon any other entity. Should "original" be understood to mean, in this case, that something just plain unique and without parallel is being presupposed? Such an assertion must be rejected. In the realm of oral tradition, there are cases in which the beginnings of the cultic, indeed the cultic itself, are to be found.

We are trying to open up the question of the cultic use of the gospels, which took place (and still takes place to this day) with finished collections of words and stories. An old definition from the end of the twelfth century says: "A book is called legendary if it has to do with the life and death of confessors and if it is read at their feasts and in the martyrs' passionaria."[72] Legends thus stand in the service of the Christian cult: they are written both for private devotion and public worship. In this regard, the *Menologia* and *Synaxaria,* along with their emendations, are highly significant and cannot be overlooked. The matter at hand now, however, is not whether the original tradition was subsequently diverted for other purposes, but what characteristics inhered in the tradition from the beginning.

It is the people and the priests of the cult site who are the immediate bearers of a legend. The case of the *Apophthegmata Patrum* is illustrative: this book, which was read aloud and dearly loved in medieval cloisters, still bears the marks of its devotional and cultic origins.[73] In the case of the gospels, the same line of reasoning can and must be applied in reverse: the lectionaries and Gospel harmonies correspond to the *Menologia* and *Synaxaria.* The way in which Tatian's *Diatessaron* originated corresponds to the way in which the gospels originated. It has long been recognized, for example, that there is no real chronology in Tatian, only a chronological framework. The same is true of the gospels, a fact known in antiquity and the Middle Ages but that seems to have been forgotten by modern Catholicism. Augustine's *De consensu evangelistarum* had profound aftereffects, and with good reason: there[74] while describing the uniqueness of the gospels, the interpretation of which was a *crux,* Augustine made a virtue of necessity by mentioning (in connection with the arrangement of events by *anticipatio*

72. J. Beleth, *De div. off.* 60 (Migne, Series Latina 202, 66). Cf. E. v. Dobschütz, s.v. "Legende" in *Realenzyklopadie für protest. Theologie und Kirche* (3 Aufl.), XI, 346.

73. After finishing the present work, I discovered that W. Bousset does briefly introduce this subject matter in the *opus postumum* that I have already cited (92): "Joannes Moschos occasionally mentions that the fathers in their cloisters read from the '*Vitae et sententiae Patrum*' (c. 55, 212). Later, when it became customary throughout Cappadocia to read the '*sacra lectiones*' at the table (Cassian, *Instit.* IV, 17), the book of the fathers would have had a role to play in those readings." It is worth pointing out that it may also be presupposed that ascetic monks read aloud at the table, and the "sentences of the fathers" may be a possibility there as well.

74. Cf. *Wiener Kirchenväterausgabe,* Bd. 43, 152f.

and *recapitulatio*) that there was no *ordo rerum gestarum*, only an *ordo recorda-tionis*. Somehow this important point was never completely lost. It is essentially immaterial that later gospel harmonizers, especially the Protestant ones, dis-avowed it.[75]

What interests us most here is the fact that the gospel harmonies result from the use of pericopes, and the gospels have to be interpreted the same way. Even the lectionaries used pericopes, often lifting stories out of their settings and telling them as if they were individual Jesus-stories. Some of their later readings were not in the first written editions of the gospels, but the old process of read-ing by pericopes brought them back to the light of day.[76] It was public reading of the gospels in early Christianity that produced such lectionaries by a process that is difficult to quantify exactly. We do not know, for example, at what point it became customary for the gospels to be read aloud in the communities. That does not mean, however, that the gospels became books of the community only after they had been fully written. The boundaries are fluid here, but even the pre-liminary stages of the gospels have to be elucidated by the use of pericopes. On the one hand the finished gospels promoted the worshiping life of the commu-nity, but on the other hand it was the worshiping life of the earliest community that brought the gospels into existence, allowed them to grow, and decisively shaped the course of their development. It is very instructive in this regard to compare the earliest gospels, which came forth from the life of a community, with the later apocryphal gospels, which lacked this anchor and thus played over into the realm of the Hellenistic novel. Yet we know nothing definite about the worshiping life of the earliest Christian communities. We cannot really imagine how lively all these things would have been within a circle of storytellers in the Christian community. But if we are to make the necessary effort to understand the earliest period in the gospel tradition, we will have to make use of hypothe-ses. We know that we cannot achieve indubitable certainty, but hypotheses will help us grasp things and see them at least generally in the right perspective.[77] Such efforts are justified by analogies from lives of the saints and from the

75. Cf. my *Der Rahmen der Geschichte Jesu*, 9ff.

76. Cf. *Der Rahmen*, esp. in the index under "Jesusperikopen" (under ὁ Ἰησοῦς or something similar in the *Codices*), and "Perikopenpraxis."

77. Theodor Zahn (*Einleitung in das Neue Testament*, 3rd ed., vol. 2 [1907], 167) makes some observant remarks about the public reading of the gospels in early Chris-tianity, but it seems to me that he does not make the necessary effort to go any further back. In a similar way, J. Haussleiter says: "It is a characteristic trait of the early Christ-ian writings that they did not intend to serve the interests of knowledge or speculation, but rather to directly promote early Christian faith and life. This purpose was achieved through the public reading of stories in the church. Every primitive Christian document for which we have evidence was connected to public reading or was used in public wor-ship in some circles somewhere for some length of time" (*Göttingen Gelehrten Anzeigen* [1898], 340). We can reason from effect to cause here: public reading of the finished gospels presupposes public reading of the developing gospels.

Apophthegmata Patrum, which were used in a cult and which still bear the marks of their cultic origin.

But we must dig deeper, not only working back from the *use* of the tradition in public cultic worship toward its *origin* in public cultic worship, but even more to the realization that this trait is inherent in the tradition itself, regardless of how it was used (not misused) later. It has already become clear that the tradition was handed on not by individuals but by a group (a people, a fellowship, a community). Something can happen to writings that originate more with individuals that can never happen to writings born in a group: the individual author, who dominates the material, can objectify it to a certain extent. Here, by contrast, there is a community that is so involved in the very existence of the writings that objectifying is out of the question from the start. The community builds itself out of traditions and records that are at work in its midst; it constitutes itself around them and is established as a community thereby. This all takes place in a kind of reciprocal action: the stronger the life of the community, the stronger the tradition that holds the community together; and as the mass of the tradition gains momentum, the community becomes more solid. Of course, there are degrees of difference here, and these remarks do not apply equally to all the folk traditions, folk books, monastic histories, and hagiographies we have considered.

A cult is not easy to identify when it is just getting started, but it can be detected at essential points in its early stages. Recall what we said about the origin of hagiographies and the folk book of Doctor Faust. There are times when we find a narrative with an agenda, a tendency, which belongs not only to a particular author, or even to the redactors, but to the very people who handed on the traditions. It seems to me that most researchers are frightened off by findings like these, which are admittedly difficult to get hold of, so they understandably revert to source criticism. They seek to determine what the original source looked like and what kind of authority it goes back to. As early as Papias and Justin, the effort was already underway to establish the reliability of the gospels. Besides, it might be objected, would not the floodgates be opened for all kinds of arbitrariness if the goal of proving the reliability of the gospels were to be abandoned? In response it must be stated that loose talk about dangerous consequences does absolutely no good at all. In a pure study of the gospels, as with other similar deposits of tradition, one often runs the risk of having apparently solid sources slip through one's fingers. Every Gospel researcher (and every scholar of legends) has to keep that possibility in view, and must get used to the fact that *non liquet* shows up much more often than the historian would like. That is no basis for skepticism—it just has to be stipulated as one of the consequences of my point of view.

At this point we have to draw our conclusions very carefully. If it has been determined that the earliest narrators of the gospel stories were not disinterested and did not maintain an objective attitude, that does not mean that the original tradition is shot through with subjectivism. In his remarks on the St. Rochus legend,

Goethe rightly saw that "contradictions did not come up, but endless variations did, which may be due to the fact that each person told a different part of the story or a different episode."[78] Martin Buber likewise recognized that "authenticity is personally attested, as each narrator speaks of 'his' rabbi or his father or teacher."[79] This method is not objective, but neither is it purely subjective: it creates a situation that transcends both of those possibilities. In his candidating lecture at Berlin on "The Implications of the Cult-historical Method for New Testament Studies," G. Bertram described the connection between community tradition and cult as follows: "In order for a document to be identified as popular, it must be . . . not only formally different from literature, suitable for a broad social class, and predisposed toward certain themes, but it must also have the inimitable characteristic of lifting reports out of the sphere of the coincidental and into the universal, making the relative absolute. This principle of folk-narration derives from primitive peoples' yearning for uncomplicated simplicity, which enables them to grasp that which is essential in an event, the ultimate significance of an occurrence."[80] Applied to the story of Jesus, this idea means the following: "Thus there arose not a portrait of a person, either objective (more or less) or subjective, but a cult narrative, which (like all folk-tradition) is basically indifferent to matters of time and place, psychology and causality, individualization and motivation, but which tends to include absolute oppositions, objectification, and standardizing." (In my opinion, Bertram should have avoided the word *objectification,* even if it is clear what he means by it, because he has explicitly rejected the idea of an "objective portrait.")

If such a connection between community folk narratives and cult does exist, then real analogies to the gospels immediately become apparent. As has already been noted, comparable documents lie within easy reach. The statement from Buber that I referred to earlier, that Hasidic narrative has the aura of holy story, is not a mere flourish but has a deep and broad background in reality, for Hasidic legend is positively saturated with cultic and mythic content.[81] Therein lies its special power; and in early Christianity too, the question of its power is essential. The Zaddik, who towers over the masses of the Hasidim, is the special favorite of heaven; through him God bestows gifts of grace on the world. Every Hasid is obligated to love and obey him, so that the Zaddik becomes a kind of mediator between God and humanity. He is not a priest or a monk; he is a layperson who is more devoted than anyone else—purely, strongly, and totally—to universal, eternal, and heavenly purposes. In a sense, there is even something like "Zaddikism": the view that the essence of piety consists in attachment to the

---

78. See above, p. 65.
79. See above, p. 66.
80. G. Bertram, *Theologische Blätter* (1923): col. 25ff.
81. Cf., in addition to Buber's aforementioned work on the great Maggid, his earlier book, *Die Legende des Baal-Schem* (1918), as well as Paul Levertoff, *Die religiöse Denkweise der Chassidim* (1918).

Zaddik. Three concentric circles spread out around him: the masses of help-seekers streaming to and fro, then the community bound to him by place and life, and finally the close spiritual circle of students and disciples. All of this depends on the relationship between the Zaddik and the community as it comes to light in their common prayers. Even if the Zaddik prays in a special place, he can still be related to his community, for a relationship like this transcends particular localities: it ultimately produces a "circle." A Jewish source states:

> On Sabbaths and holidays the hasidim partake of a 'sacred meal' at the table of the Zaddik. Silence prevails during the meal, although from time to time the Zaddik "speaks Torah," i.e., expounds on the biblical text for the day. The Zaddik eats very little of the fare; most of it is shared among the guests. The hasidim call the table of the Zaddik "the altar of God," and the meal "a sacrifice to God." If the Zaddik enjoys some of the food, he is a high priest offering a sacrifice to God. After the meal the hasidim gather to linger in conversation about their Zaddik, weighing every word he spoke, interpreting every gesture he made and every look they saw in his eyes, and trying to fathom all the mysterious significance of their observations. During this conversation they all sit very close together; when one speaks, the others hang on his every word. Any distinction between great and small, rich or poor, is completely erased.[82]

The exact words spoken by the Zaddik are not what matter most, and almost no regard is given to refined or deliberative conversation. Instead, Hasidic literature repeatedly asserts that one should "learn from every member of the Zaddik." Notice here the influence the Zaddik exerts over his circle: he is a cult personality in his own lifetime.

We turn then to Jesus and his disciples. Should things be any different here? Is there some circuit breaker that cuts Jesus and his disciples off from what we have been discussing? In his book *The Idea of the Holy,* Rudolf Otto has remarked upon the "numinous impact of Jesus upon his disciples,"[83] but wide circles of critical theology have regarded Otto's point as unfounded. In my judgment, the Hasidic tradition offers a good illustration—and one which is especially instructive because it can be checked—of the fact that the range of possible analogies must be cast more widely than critics usually allow. In both cases, "the center is always the man himself" (as Otto puts it), "a saint in his own lifetime."

The form of the Hasidic tradition also matches that of the Gospel tradition. Jesus was just like a Zaddik to his community and to his disciples, not only in his lifetime but also as the exalted one, the spiritual one, the πνεῦμα of his community become present to his disciples. And what is the content of the cult-legend? Sayings and miracle stories in both cases! Hasidism, and Zaddikism in

82. Levertoff, *Die religiöse Denkweise der Chassidim,* 101.
83. Rudolf Otto, *The Idea of the Holy,* trans. J. W. Harvey (Oxford, 1976), 159.

particular, is rife with miracle stories. In addition, a Zaddik like Baal-Shem has (like all primary religious figures) highly developed abilities in speaking in parables. Martin Buber, who brought this tradition to life for us, sees it as the ultimate extant form of Jewish myth and as part of a chain that includes the story of Jesus as well: a "school" is "born, carrying along the greatest of the Nazarenes and creating his legend, the greatest triumph of all for myth."[84] Other scholars have also emphasized the similarity to the gospels. Levertoff, who was (not coincidentally) a missionary to Jews, found here an important starting-point for his missionary efforts: "If we can just get a hasidic Jew to read the gospels, we can expect them to make a powerful impression on him." And his assessment of the Hasidic legends applies equally well to the gospels: "The stylus seems to have broken under the strain of making a very bold stroke; it is not that the Zaddik is inaccessible because the portrait of him is scanty—the portrait of him is scanty because he is inaccessible."[85]

Scholars dispute the extent to which the Jesus traditions have a mythic character. Certainly the story of Jesus eventually appears as a Christ-myth in the gospels, but it did not originate as such.[86] The Hasidic legends likewise contain episodes that began as individual pieces of tradition. The worshiping, cultic character of these two traditions is more palpable, and this character continues to persist even after the individual pieces of cultic content have been laid bare by the work of rational examination. There is no exact parallel in the Hasidic legends, however, for the way in which specific historical dates attached themselves to the Christ myth and cult. These dates carried weight and left their own special mark even though they originated in the life of the primitive Christian community. We ought not to undervalue Hasidism, but we do have to ask at this point about the special, unsurpassable δύναμις of primitive Christianity, and we have to refer to primitive Christian eschatology for an answer.[87] All of this combined with myth and cult to produce the gospels.[88]

84. M. Buber, *Die Legende des Baal-Schem* (1918), ix.

85. P. Levertoff, *Die religiöse Denkweise der Chassidim* (1918), 103.

86. M. Dibelius, *From Tradition to Gospel*, 278–79.

87. Cf. my essay "Eschatologie und Mystik im Urchristentum," *ZNW* 23 (1922): 277ff. M. Buber also opens up the problem of eschatology and evaluates it *in malam partem;* see his preface to *Der grosse Maggid* (xxiv).

88. I am well aware that these remarks offer little more than a marginal note on questions that are hotly disputed. According to R. Bultmann (*History of the Synoptic Tradition*), "the genre of the Gospels presupposes the Christ cult and myth and is a creation of Hellenistic Christianity." Of course, my remarks do not apply to the preliminary stages of the gospels. But it seems to me that Bultmann overlooks the essential beginnings of something that later comes to constitute the Christ cult, after it has been saturated with Hellenistic content: in addition to what has been said above about the influence of Jesus on his contemporaries, the complex of Easter stories has to be remembered here, even if an elusive or even insoluble X does lie behind it. It further seems to me that Bultmann does not quite rightly evaluate the connection between

By this point it ought to be clear that a cult legend has to be read and evaluated in a particular way, and may I say that a degree of tact is called for here, the lack of which can neutralize the entire project and lead a scholar into serious mistakes. If we are obsessed with the idea of getting results that are totally logical, then our results will be totally logical—and utterly negative. There are certain undeniable facts here that simply must be pointed out. Over and over again in the course of historical Jesus research, aspects of the portrait of Jesus that had been regarded as essential (or maybe even as the only ones available) have been wiped out by succeeding generations of scholars. Currently, for example, there is renewed debate over the old question of whether and to what extent Jesus was eschatological. Those who deny the historicity of Jesus have added up all these results of gospel criticism and have come up with a big zero. In the process, each scholar (or, better, each interpreter) has extracted a picture of Jesus from the cult legend. It simply cannot be denied that imponderables resonate here and that these imponderables are more important to understanding the history than many supposedly "precise" methods.

More recent and radical Jesus researchers, who make rigorous use of form-critical and cult-historical methods in order to unravel what is "original," have to work all the time (if they are honest) with words like "perhaps," "probably," "possibly," "probably not," "obviously," and so on. It is inherent in the esoteric properties of the gospels—since they are so definitely cultic—that a good deal

---

community and cult tradition. M. Dibelius (*From Tradition to Gospel*) draws the lines less sharply than Bultmann. His overall picture is less garishly lit and less sharply contoured than Bultmann's, and it appears to me to be more correct.

G. Bertram has recently produced a very impressive, if not always clear and complete, work on the importance of the cult-historical viewpoint for the emergence of the earliest (not just the Hellenistic) community and its tradition (*Die Leidensgeschichte Jesu und der Christus-kult,* 1922). In my opinion, A. Jülicher correctly points out that Bertram uses an "uncommonly broad concept of cult," which basically means that he defines piety differently, so that the "distance between Bertram and most scholars is in principle a modest one." As important as this objection is, it would be deplorable to sharply criticize and discredit a novel investigation into the importance of the cult-history question just because that investigation is not completely successful. Jülicher's methodology is too individualistic to contest Bertram's construction ("The piety of the community," writes Jülicher, meaning the cult, "if it really is something special, is rooted in the tradition only through the witness of individuals, and individuals are always the controlling influence") (*Theologischer Literaturzeitung* (1923), 9ff). It is symptomatic that Martin Werner of Bonn makes some very spirited remarks in opposition to Jülicher (cf. *Kirchenblatt für die reformierte Schweiz* (1923), 33ff), pointing out in particular the great distance between the new perspective and the older "critical" one. He regards the older view as a harbinger of Catholicism and calls the "utter pitifulness and doubtfulness of such 'final solutions'" an "intellectual embarrassment" (?!). It seems to me that the point about Catholicism is not completely mistaken; but shouldn't we beware lest such remarks become self-fulfilling prophecies?

will always have to remain uncertain. But this fact by no means entails that all is lost, as the analogies to the gospels in other cult legends have clearly shown. Even here one could employ methods of criticism that would leave no remainder— but the historical picture would still rest on a cult legend. Think of the accounts of the saint from Assisi, or of the Hasidic legends, which we explored last of all. In contrast to the ancient rabbinic traditions (which have also been compared with the gospels),[89] the production, collection, and outlook of the Hasidic tradition rests not with learned individuals but with a people, a people who gathered themselves as a community around their Zaddik.

Martin Buber had it right when he put it this way in the introduction to his book on Baal-Shem: "I do not recite dates and events, as if to put together a biography of Baal-Shem. I construct his life out of his legend, in which reside the dreams and longings of a people." If we regard the gospels from this perspective, do they lose their historical tangibility? Not in my opinion. The people as a community became bearers and creators of the tradition, and this certifies its content. A tradition that originated with an individual, by contrast, would have gotten the details right (like the minutes of a business meeting) but would have missed the big picture. The gospels, I thus conclude, are cultic folk books, or else folk cult-books.

89. See above, p. 16. Even if M. Dibelius is right that the rabbinic tradition stands out from the gospels because it is defined by Law, the rabbinic tradition is still different from Hasidic legends. Hasidism is the opposite pole of rabbinism.

PART THREE

ON THE PROBLEM OF THE LITERARY CHARACTER OF THE GOSPELS: THE HISTORY OF RELIGIONS AND THEOLOGICAL QUESTION.

The analogies to the gospels that we have found among folk books and legends can be multiplied almost indefinitely. It would be most stimulating, for example, to look into legends about the so-called founders[1] of other religions, the content of which would surely be relevant to our picture of Jesus. Doubtless our method would produce results in the stories of the Buddha and Mohammed, especially the *Hadith*. It appears to me, however, that nothing new (beyond what is already known) can be extracted from the traditions with which I have been working here. In every case we have had to deal with (as Gunkel puts it) the *"Sitz im Leben,"*[2] so that contemporaneous parallels with the gospels are not the most important ones. Of course, we should never underestimate the significance of rabbinic literature for understanding the gospels and the New Testament, but at the end of the day we are forced to conclude that the more recent Hasidic material is of greater value in explaining the form of the gospels. In my opinion, a comparison between primitive Christian forms of storytelling and contemporaneous Jewish forms sheds more light on the individual pieces of the gospel tradition than on the collected gospels as wholes.[3] In the course of our investigations, we also encountered the idea that the rabbinic anecdotes must be brought into the picture.

It was our guiding purpose all along to interact specifically with all previous attempts to understand the gospels in the framework of general history of literature. Overall, very many of these efforts are rather good, although we did find a few bad cases that could not withstand close examination. In addition, we often found studies and investigations that evinced an attitude that was not exactly congenial toward the contents of the gospels. The range of assertions and counter-assertions in these literary-historical methodologies is, by any standard,

1. Jesus really should not be referred to as a "founder" of a religion. Unlike Mohammed, Jesus did not organize a church or establish a cult. To impute such actions to him is Pelagian—and wrong.
2. Cf. H. Gunkel, *Reden und Aufsätze* (1913), 33. The expression *Sitz im Leben* appears in *Theologische Rundschau* (1917), 269, with reference to the "ancient literary genre." *Primitive* would be a better word than *ancient*.
3. The prime example here is the work of P. Fiebig. The material Fiebig has already presented is more important than that with which he proposes to continue. The problem of the rabbinic material has also been noted in works by M. Dibelius and R. Bultmann.

very broad. As far back as Justin, for example, the assertion was made (and is still being made today) that the gospels are "memorabilia" like the work of the same title by Xenophon. How blithely the tradition of a particular cult is linked up with the work of a scholar! The Gospel of John, which stems from a circle of disciples, is taken for a clumsy compilation, on the level of Diogenes Laertius and his lives of philosophers! Collections of parenetic material like the Sermon on the Mount are regarded as speeches like those created by Thucydides! Luke is supposedly a parallel to Polybius and a precursor to Eusebius! It is actually believed that the historical worth of the gospels can be measured by such comparisons. Yet the more honestly and closely we work with the details, the more we see that the evangelists—even Luke—are quite far removed from the ideals of documentary historians.

But what happens instead? On and on goes the search goes for "better" sources, further and further back, with hypotheses about "Ur-Luke" or "Ur-Mark." In the process, people—I refer here to those scholars who have to work their way diligently through all the details of these elaborate hypotheses—become every bit as unproductive as the ideas they are trying to get to the bottom of. How many hypotheses about sources and interpolations have been advanced, only to disappear again in the blink of an eye! Yet even these unsuccessful efforts do accomplish something, if only to show that a deficient methodology leads to nothing but absurdity, as indeed it must. Wendling's meticulous studies of Ur-Mark at least had the benefit of forcing him to look more closely at Mark, the oldest gospel, and Wellhausen's remarks about Mark did contain the germ of a better method for solving these problems. Spitta's grand revision of synoptic theory rightly caught the attention of Johannes Weiss, the most prominent advocate of the Markan hypothesis. Both of these scholars employed essentially the same literary-critical method, and Spitta used it so forcefully that J. Weiss was almost ready to capitulate. E. Klostermann, who adopted the Markan hypothesis, felt that he had to take account of Spitta's studies in his commentary on Luke.

Yet full emphasis must be squarely placed on this important point: Spitta can be refuted only if the "framework of the story" upon which he builds is exposed as completely sterile. Then and only then can another viewpoint take over, as indeed another viewpoint has taken over in these pages. We have had to carry on a vigorous fight against heavily fortified positions, because the general picture of the literary and religious history of primitive Christianity currently suffers from all kinds of prejudices and distortions that will not go away quietly. Gospel research now stands under an unlucky star of impressionism and caprice. Both theological and philological study (theology leads the way; philology follows along behind—most of the time too closely) are following a path between Catholicism and mythologization, between the view that myth and cult are incompatible with history and the view that myth and cult are identical with history. A middle way, trying to split the difference between positive and negative, calls for a kind of tentative vacillation: "scientific" pretexts are the currency in which business has to be transacted. In this way a scholar learns just as much from the assertions of Arthur Drews as from Catholic interpretations.

Obviously nothing at all is accomplished by simply following the golden mean. Unless it can somehow be possible to measure the exact distance between right and left, then the correct course must be radical and positive and must make a sharp, clean cut. The real argument is not between Catholicism and Protestantism in the usual sense, because for too long Protestantism has not been in earnest about the true way. Nor is the argument between right-wing (conservative, orthodox) and left-wing (liberal, critical) theologies. In this study I have learned just as much from right-wing theologians like Theodor Zahn and A. Schlatter as I have from those on the left, and at various times I have rejected opinions on both sides. And the real argument is also not between theology and philology: it involves both theologians like Spitta, Harnack, and Bousset and philologists like Wendling, Eduard Meyer, and Reitzenstein.

This analysis of the methodological dilemma is not as important, however, as the observation that recognizing the *Sitz im Leben* has an immediate impact on the study of the gospels. It means that simple questions about sources must not be overly exaggerated. The gospels must be understood as originating in early Christianity and as being imprinted by the early Christian community in the same way that the *Apophthegmata Patrum* arose from ascetic monasticism, the Francis legend from the Franciscan movement, and the Hasidic legends from Hasidism. Questions about sources are not the most important point; what matters most is recognizing that the gospels are the expression of a religious fact, a religious movement.

Perhaps this is the point at which I may touch upon a related matter in theological education: in every university program I know of, as soon as young theology students have read the Synoptic Gospels, they are told that they should turn to the "sources" for the story of Jesus. That may be feasible if the interpreter knows how to extract original sources through a purely logical process of literary criticism. But form-critical and cult-historical methods will not allow us to give students this familiar advice. Whoever wants to go deeply into the gospels—and here there is no distinction between John and the Synoptics—must first acquire a conception of early Christianity. To that end other parts of the New Testament have to be introduced, principally the Letters of Paul and the Catholic Epistles.

It can be shown that it is a mistake to lift "sources" out of the gospels by means of periodizing devices and psychologizing interpretations, as if it were simply a matter of stripping off coats of paint. There is, by contrast, nothing psychological or ornamental about a genuine folk-tradition. Students of the gospels have to learn that there is no such thing as a life of Jesus, such as J. Lepsius wrote as recently as 1917–18. Teachers have to realize that we cannot talk about the journeys of Jesus or about his psychological development. And writers must understand that we may not write novels about Jesus either, no matter how convincing the milieu may be, as it is for example in the most recent Jesus novel by

Else Zurhellen-Pfleiderer (1922). The cultic content of the gospels gets buried alive in a novel. The pearls of the individual gospel traditions, which sparkle with variety when loosely strung together, get trampled into a paste and molded into a different entity. The material of the pearls is not totally lost, but their beauty is. Read any Jesus novel—you will gladly go back to reading the gospels.

Our comparative studies have shown that the real question has nothing to do with simply calling attention to the idea of a "gospel" with popular and cultic characteristics. The technical term εὐαγγέλιον comes nowhere close to answering the question we are concerned with here. For that term was used in a sacral context within the Roman imperial cult as well as in Philostratus's *Life of Apollonius of Tyana,* where it describes the arrival of Apollonius himself (I.28). Thus the gospel-sayings, stories, and books that we are concerned with here are to be found in the religious rather than the literary realm. But now we know to look for the popular and cultic content! That is the conclusion to which all of our investigations have led us.

It takes no special insight into the nature of the gospels to see that they are devotional, practical, plain, and popular. But the force of the expression "popular" can be lost through overuse. It seems to me that the word carries two connotations: first, it can mean "easy to understand," or "simple," a meaning that has no application at all to the gospels. Some individualistic biographies, which we have differentiated from the gospels, are popular in that sense of the word. But it is entirely different to use the word *popular* in the second sense: "aboriginal" or "native" (like a folk song). Only then does it become plain why the gospels, like other native literature, are nonchronological, nonpsychological, and nonpragmatic.

Yet this does not diminish the basic Palestinian aroma of the earliest settings, for that aroma does not arise from the pieces of the framework. There is no topography, in the proper sense of that word, in the gospels. This point is essential to refuting those who dispute the historicity of Jesus—Bruno Bauer, Albert Kalthoff, and others who argue that since place designations in the gospels have no historical value, there is no trace of local color in the gospels at all. These scholars have put their finger on a tender spot, but what about specific designations like Capernaum and Jerusalem? Caution is called for here: both of these places are foci not only for the activities of Jesus but also for the collection of traditions about him.[4] I calculate that more traditions gathered around Capernaum than actually belonged there. It is highly illustrative that the story of the young man at Nain was also localized at Capernaum: the Old Latin manuscript of Luke 7:11 reads *capharnaum.* If we fail to recognize this characteristic of the gospel tradition and end up talking about the "places and paths of Jesus"

---

4. A methodologically solid argument against A. Kalthoff has been laid down by M. Bruckner in *Das fünfte Evangelium (Das heilige Land),* 1910. He says everything that needs to be said about this question.

on the basis of secondary framing pieces, we will be chasing after a level of perception that is simply not available to us.[5]

It seems to me that the concept of "popular" must be filled with content of
this sort. Nothing more stands to be gained by monotonously repeating the assertion that since the gospels are popular, they are not literary. We have shown
again and again that the gospels have nothing at all to do with contemporaneous
high literature. The mere fact that they stand outside the Attic revival of those
days should suffice to show the error of that idea, which, unfortunately, we have
encountered all too often in these pages. The gospels belong, instead, to the low
literature. Just like high literature, this kind of literature is also "meant for a
definite 'public' and is not written merely for the circle of the author's acquain-
tances. On this point a distinction can be made between low literature and writings which are entirely private. This distinction can be easily illustrated by the
fact that nowadays publications like tracts, popular calendars, club brochures
and novellas are distinguished from mere personal notes and from mechanically
duplicated documents, even those run off 'in manuscript form.' Only the former
are professionally published."[6] M. Dibelius was right to put this statement on the
opening page of *From Tradition to Gospel.* For if the art of book printing had
existed in the Roman Empire, the gospels would surely have come out in printed
form like German folk books and books of legends, and not in manuscript.[7] It is
precisely the analogies that we have placed alongside the gospels that are most
suited to determining the *Sitz im Leben* based on the content.[8]

5. Here I must agree completely with R. Bultmann's review of G. Dalman, *Orte
und Wege Jesu;* cf. *Theologische Blätter* (1923): 123ff.

6. M. Dibelius, *From Tradition to Gospel,* 1–2.

7. W. Wrede is often too doctrinaire in his judgments, but he is completely right
to stress that the gospels stand at some remove from high literature while being closely
connected to low literature. Cf. esp. W. Wrede, *Die Entstehung der Schriften des Neuen
Testaments* (1907).

8. A. Deissmann has done us the great service of repeatedly pointing out the popular character of the early Christian writings. He offers a comprehensive summary of his
perspective in the third major section of his book *Light from the Ancient East,* 2nd and
3rd eds. (1909), 100–183. Differentiating between genuine letters and literary epistles,
Deissmann limits himself to looking at early Christian letters, illustrating them with
examples of "twenty-one original ancient non-literary letters." But the gospel documents
are quite a different matter, and nonliterary sources like papyri, ostraca, and inscriptions (only the last of which falls within the purview of *Light from the Ancient East*)
shed no light at all on the process by which the gospels were handed down. Deissmann
shows his awareness of this fact when he poses the problem of the literary evolution of
Christianity (as Franz Overbeck has so aptly put it), but then, after discussing the difference between letters and epistles, Deissmann tries to describe the "literary evolution
of early Christianity" and expresses the feeling that the question cannot be settled apart
from knowledge of the inscriptions "as well as the papyri and ostraca" (182). But to
understand the gospels it is essential to draw on low literature. Deissmann allows for
this possibility, at least to the extent that he "eagerly awaits" the appearance of Paul

Thus far we have discussed the gospels per se, touching only now and then on questions about the relationship of the first three gospels to the fourth. We have also only occasionally addressed the special case of the third evangelist. In addition, we have compared only the completed gospels as wholes with other finished literary products, giving but cursory attention to analogies for the individual pieces themselves. Of course, the various genres within the gospels also have their own analogies according to their inherent structures. How multiform, for example, are the sayings of Jesus! They belong more to the genre of short poetry (e.g., epigrams, similes, prophetic utterances, riddles) than to that of extended prose (e.g., sentences, parables, apocalypses, allegories). In addition, there are also dialogues in the form of controversy stories.[9] The narratives are similar to the sayings, except that an important distinction has to be made. The so-called *apophthegmata,* sayings that are set in a framework, constitute that distinction. Central to the narratives are the miracle stories, which vary so much

---

Wendland's work, *Die urchristlichen Literaturformen.* As a matter of fact, Wendland did understand the literary evolution of early Christianity quite clearly and correctly, and we have made explicit use of his views in the pages above. It is from his work (which had not yet appeared when the 2nd and 3rd editions of *Light from the Ancient East* were published) that we have taken the outline of a form-critical method for studying the gospels.

I received the 4th edition of Deissmann's *Light from the Ancient East* only after the present manuscript was completed. The third major section, to which I have referred above, is virtually unchanged, except that the discussion has been enhanced by the addition of five more ancient letters. Deissmann shows no sign of recognizing that since 1909 there has been a good deal of discussion about his rather strongly defined concept of "early Christian folk-books," but his knowledge of the research on the genre of the gospels is valuable. He rightly distances himself from H. Windisch's opinion that his 1895 "genre study" of letters and epistles has survived the "impact" of Gunkel. For my part, I have already noted above (p. 41n. 21.) that Windisch did not get the priority relationships quite right. In the "Addenda and Corrections" (p. 447), Deissmann mentions an essay by M. Albertz in *Ev. Kirchenblatt für Schlesien* 24 (1921), 326ff, calling it a contribution "to form-critical research." This essay, in which Albertz defines his priorities over against R. Bultmann (but why isn't M. Dibelius mentioned as well since his 1919 book had appeared by this time?), is difficult to grasp, more difficult at least than other form-critical works. What concerns us here is the question of analogies to the gospels. P. Wendland's informative study, which Deissmann said in his 2nd and 3rd editions he was "eagerly awaiting," is barely mentioned in the 4th edition. But at least the 4th edition amends the sentence, "Only a few scholars had a good feel for the whole problem of a close literary-critical examination of early Christianity" with the insertion of the adverb, "formerly." This change brings the book up to date.

One thing must be stated in conclusion: as long as anything is possible in gospel studies (i.e., as long as it is still possible to reach conclusions like those of Eduard Meyer, which we have analyzed above), Deissmann's strong appeal for attention to the popular character of the gospels will continue to have value, even if he himself does not quite understand what that means.

9. Cf. here esp. M. Albertz, *Die synoptischen Streitgespräche* (1921).

that they almost cannot be subsumed under one single literary rubric: some have the abbreviated form of a paradigm; others, the extended form of a novella. Thus, they can be viewed and evaluated from various perspectives. In fact, there is a wide variety of possibilities here, each one with its own legitimate claim; and at this point the conversation is still going on, as analogies from other regions of literary history are undergoing various kinds of sifting and evaluation.

In the present work, our prime concern has been the redaction of the traditional material, and we believe that we have found useful guiding principles for its assessment in the general history of literature. It is especially instructive to note that despite their common outlook, each of the gospels has been redacted in a different way. The constraint of the material, which is characteristic of all oral tradition, steadily declines, and the freedom of the authorial personality steadily increases. That which was completely absent or only barely present at the beginning of the gospel tradition steps into the foreground in the later gospels (in some respects the Gospel of John belongs with the apocryphal gospels). The beginnings of a style that features the authorial "I" as well as embellishments and details of psychological interest can be discerned. Such is the way that leads from the preliminary stages of the oral tradition to Mark and Matthew, then to Luke, and subsequently to John and the apocryphal gospels.[10] This course of events represents a progressive secularization of the gospels.

But that is not all that needs to be said. The fourth evangelist is not quite as secularized as the authors of the apocryphal gospels (all of whom are virtually unknown to us). Instead, he creates an utterly esoteric gospel, which, even though it is a collection, is still distinguished from the Synoptics in the way it uses pericopes. Is the Gospel of John basically a book of pericopes? Is it essentially a popular gospel? It almost appears as if the Gospel of John may have broken the mold for a gospel and produced a more unified concept of a great drama. This "unworldly" gospel is remarkably secular.[11] The Gospel of Luke is unmistakable in this regard. This study has repeatedly shown that Luke displays the

10. This has been nicely sketched out by P. Wendland, *Die urchristlichen Literaturformen,* 2nd and 3rd eds. (1912), 258ff.

11. I have only belatedly become acquainted with H. Windisch's essay, "Der johanneischen Erzählungstil," which is also in the Gunkel Festschrift book in which "Die Stellung" first appeared, and I am pleased that the questions I am posing here receive a very thorough treatment there. The important question of the literary character of the Gospel of John is taken in hand to very good effect, and "the great paradox of this Gospel," which I have briefly mentioned above, is very closely investigated. Cf. in this regard A. Deissmann, *Light from the Ancient East,* 2nd and 3rd eds., (1909), 180f: "In spite of the Logos in the opening lines, the Gospel of John is completely popular." In the 4th edition of 1923, a new footnote appears on p. 211: "This sentence is obviously a very brief formulation of an entire project which has kept me busy for three decades. The widely held and increasingly dominant view is that the Gospel of John is aristocratic and doctrinaire, but we must reckon seriously with the realization that it still has a popular and cultic character."

rudiments of being a genuine member of the literati. Of all the documents in the New Testament, his style shows the strongest signs of worldly culture. His prologue has the format of a document from contemporaneous world literature, and he makes a show of his authorial "I," but his efforts turn out most unhappily. Elsewhere I have examined Luke's redactional work in detail,[12] and I have arrived at the conclusion that Luke's abilities were strangely unequal to his intentions, that the material imposed restrictions on him. Thus, the high opinion of Luke's work that is so widely held may be sorely in need of correction.

The strongest corroboration for this thesis of mine comes from Franz Overbeck's many publications on the Synoptic Problem.[13] Overbeck has been working on these issues for some years and is, in a word, anti-Luke. A very few sentences may illustrate:

> Nothing is more indicative of Luke's conception of the gospel story, insofar as he sets a goal for historiography, than the fact that he has the idea of writing Acts as a sequel to his Gospel. In spectacularly bad taste Luke attempts to carry out an utterly outrageous pretense. . . . The third evangelist completely fails to achieve his purpose, which was to shape the material of the gospel tradition into historiography—a dilettante's idea, and small wonder that the dilettante betrays himself. . . . And yet Luke is often praised as a skilled author. He is that, but he exercises his skill on reluctant material and so comes to grief. Luke treats as history that which was not history and was not handed down as history. But he respects the tradition, and thus a chasm yawns open between the traditional material and the form in which he wants to put it. . . . As a matter of fact the prologue to Luke's Gospel is one of those places in the New Testament where the world shows through most clearly; it can be said that in Luke's prologue the New Testament is at its most secular.[14]

I know of no one who recognized and wanted to resolve the history of religions and theological problem as much as Overbeck. It is no whim of fancy or vague impressionism to follow him into his passionate declarations (Overbeck the critic was something of an enthusiast) and to find confirmed therein the results of one's own lengthy and detailed studies, because Overbeck himself has provided both a clear statement of the problem and solid work on it in his precise and well-received 1882 essay entitled, "On the Beginnings of Patristic Literature."[15] Once again, I would prefer to quote his polished and weighty prose rather than try to put into my own words what he has said so much better: "Since

---

12. See my *Der Rahmen der Geschichte Jesu,* esp. p. 316.

13. G. A. Bernoulli, ed. *Christentum und Kultur: Gedanken und Anmerkungen zur modernen Theologie von Franz Overbeck* (1919), 80–82.

14. Ibid., 78–79.

15. F. Overbeck, "Über die Anfänge der patristischen Literatur," *Historische Zeitschrift* (1882): 417–72.

the history of a literature is in its forms, all genuine literary history must be form-critical."[16] For Overbeck, the decisive point is his concept of a "primitive Christian literature" that died out very early and thus had nothing in common with later patristic literature. A gospel is a form that disappeared after a very specific point in the history of the Christian church, and it is wrong to see the beginning of church historiography in the Acts of the Apostles, since none of the patristic writers took up the theme of the gospels and Acts. Eusebius did not see himself as some sort of sequel writer. It is therefore not possible to trace the form of Eusebius's *Ecclesiastical History* back to the gospels and Acts.

The process of recognizing the uniqueness of "primitive Christian literature" is beset with great difficulties. Overbeck has aptly remarked: "When this primitive Christian literature is described, with all the highly unusual conditions of its existence, preservation, and survival, not to mention its special form, it becomes clear that the literary-critical problems are profound. The depth of these problems means that literary criticism faces a task that, it just so happens, shares all the difficulties of paleontology."[17] It seems to me that New Testament scholarship has, to its own detriment, repressed and forgotten insights like these. It is still possible, for example, for a historian to be praised[18] for having a healthy, naïve, and prejudiced confidence in the oldest gospel, as if that kind of approach

16. Ibid., 423.

17. Ibid., 442.

18. So Hans Lietzmann in *Historische Zeitschrift* (1922): 104, with reference to the portrait of Jesus offered by Eduard Meyer. There is a noticeable dissonance between Lietzmann's opinion in the 1922 *Historische Zeitschrift* and that of Overbeck in the 1882 volume of the same journal!

I recently received a fresh reminder of how necessary it is to keep abreast even of studies that are of deficient quality. Just before this manuscript went to press, a copy of Gustav Lippert, *Pilatus als Richter* (Wien, 1923) arrived. Lippert, who serves as counsel to the Higher Administrative Court of Austria, applies his judicial experience to the gospels, treating them as official records of the proceedings against Jesus. The book, which is "respectfully dedicated to that master of Gospel scholarship, Adolf von Harnack," expresses a modern jurist's assessment of the conduct of Pilate (a "colleague" of the author) "in this the most memorable trial of all." The author is convinced that the works of R. A. Hoffmann, Friedrich Spitta, B. Weiss, J. Wellhausen, and Emil Wendling have produced sure results with their exposition of primitive Christianity (in my opinion, this selection of scholars is downright arbitrary and certainly not agreeable to everyone). More than once, Luke is singled out for praise because he "based his work on thorough historical research and confirmation." "There is also a possibility that perhaps the author of L (= Ur-Luke) or even Luke himself, who was a traveling companion of Paul and went to Palestine in 58–60 CE, may have had access to an official record," and so on and so forth. All of this is based on gospel scholarship that is not exactly up-to-date. What about the "paleontology" of the gospels? Lippert the jurist seems even less aware than his theological informants are that the origins of the Jesus tradition were not in one or more individual documents by some writer or other, but rather in a multitude of separate traditions of the Christian community.

were the on the level of Overbeck's gifted expertise. It is incomprehensible that while Overbeck's "famous" essay can be praised in theological and philological circles, no one ever thinks of accepting his conclusions.

Lately, there has been more work on the "paleontology" of the gospels, that is, the study of their preliminary stages; and all the impulses of genre criticism have become operative. Gunkel has given us the best example in the field of Old Testament. His method is rather intricate, but the material he investigates is extensive and simple. Even though we stand outside it, we can, with proper care, detect the shape of an esoteric tradition. But our method is even simpler. In my opinion, the various parallels adduced here lay down definite ground rules, sharpening the eye for that which is unique to primitive Christianity, that which Luke tried to break through with his secular aspirations. Primitive Christianity was, on the whole, unsecular, a fact that is significant for the study of its literary forms. Form-critical methodology is thus a theological matter. The larger philosophical question about content and form is transformed into a theological question about God and the world, about Christianity and culture. Radical and positive study of the gospels is a function of the central theological issue.

INDEX

Ahikar, 14–16, 68
apocalyptic, 22, 25–26, 27
apocryphal acts, 4, 29, 32
apophthegmata, 4, 34, 56, 82
Apophthegmata Patrum, 22, 56–58, 69, 71, 79
Arrian, 4

Bauer, Bruno, 80
biography: ancient, 32–33; Greek, 3–5; peripatetic, 11–13
birth narratives, 11
Bousset, W., 15n. 41, 22, 40–41, 55, 57n. 55, 79
Buber, Martin, 66, 72, 74, 76
Bultmann, Rudolf, 7, 25, 41, 68

Callisthenes, 4
canonization, 21, 30–31
chreiai, 19, 34, 43–44, 68
cult: legend, 27, 33, 53–54, 68–69, 72–76; tradition, 30, 52, 66, 68, 71, 74

De consensu evangelistarum (Augustine), 69
Deissmann, Adolf, 81n. 8
Demonax (Lucian), 19
Diatessaron (Tatian), 69
Dibelius, Martin, 7, 16, 18, 19, 21, 41, 81
Diogenes Laertius, 5, 78
Doktor Faust, 45–51, 56

Elephantine papyri, 14
Epictetus, 4
Epictetus (Arrian), 3, 6
Eusebius, 5, 42, 78, 85

folk book, 12, 13, 14–15, 27, 33, 34, 35, 37, 48, 52, 62, 66, 71, 76
form criticism, 41, 58, 62, 75, 79, 82n. 8, 86
Francis of Assisi, 60–64, 79

Gospels: gospel tradition, 16, 21, 44, 70–71; preliminary stages of, 5, 16, 21, 36, 42, 45, 54, 56, 70, 86
Gressmann, H., 14–15, 21
Gunkel, Hermann, 39–41, 77, 86

hagiography, 20, 52–54, 71
Harnack, Adolf von, 7, 42, 79
Heinrici, C. F. G., 4
Hellenism and Judaism, 13, 17, 18
high literature, 9, 10, 11, 13, 19, 27, 33, 55, 81
Historia Lausiaca (Palladius), 12n. 36, 20, 55–56
Historia Monachorum (Rufinus), 12n. 36, 55
historiography: Greek, 17–18; Jewish, 17–18, 27n. 1
Holl, K., 12n. 36, 29

"I" (literary/authorial personality), 6, 17–18, 34, 56, 83–84

Jesus, 7, 8, 23, 24, 73, 74, 79, 82
John, Gospel of, 18, 19, 20, 21, 22, 27, 30, 78, 83
Judaism and Hellenism, 13, 17, 18
Justin, 8, 9, 10, 30, 71, 78
Jülicher, A., 24

Leo, F., 11
Lietzmann, Hans, 22, 85n. 18
Life of Apollonius of Tyana (Philostratus), 3, 19, 20, 34–36, 80
Life of St. Simeon Stylites (Antony), 22
low literature, 10, 12, 13, 18, 19, 20, 27, 33, 55, 81
Luke: evangelist, 5, 42–43, 59, 84; gospel of, 5, 6, 11, 18, 22, 27, 50, 54, 55–56, 63, 64, 78, 83

Mark: evangelist, 10, 42–45, 68; gospel
    of, 5, 7, 9, 10, 11, 18, 19, 22, 24,
    48, 50, 54, 64, 83
martyr acts, 29–30, 32
Matthew: evangelist, 43, 44; gospel of,
    5, 6, 11, 18, 22, 30, 50, 54, 83
Memorabilia (Xenophon), 3, 4, 6–10
memoirs, 6–10
Meyer, Arnold, 21
Meyer, Eduard, 9, 35, 42, 79
Michaelis, Wilhelm, 23–24
Moiragenes, 10, 34
monastic histories, 55, 71

Old Testament, 17, 39–40
Otto, Rudolf, 22–23, 73
Overbeck, Franz, 84–86

Papias, 9, 10, 71
paradigms, 19
pericopes, 70
Peter, 9, 10
Philostratus, 4
Polybius, 5, 17, 42, 78

Q, 25

Reitzenstein, Richard, 12n. 36, 55, 79

Sadhu, 23–24
Schlatter, A., 17, 53n. 47, 79
secularization, 83–86
Sitz im Leben, 77, 79, 81
Socrates, 4, 7, 8, 9
Soden, Hans von, 22, 25
Spitta, F., 48, 61, 78, 79
Streeter, B. H., 23

Thucydides, 18, 78
tradition: gospel, 5, 8–9, 15–16, 24, 41,
    44, 60, 67, 83; oral, 16, 22, 35,
    37–42, 45, 47, 56, 57n. 56, 64, 65,
    66, 69, 76, 83; rabbinic, 16–17

Votaw, Clyde Weber, 3–4

Weiss, Johannes, 6, 11, 12, 13, 18, 78
Wendland, P., 6, 20, 83n. 10
Wrede, William, 24, 81n. 7

Xenophon, 4, 6, 10

Zahn, Theodor, 8, 9, 17, 18, 39, 70n. 77, 79